# information communication & technology
## for AQA APPLIED AS
### single award

**Barbara Wilson** ◄

Consultant: Steve Bachrach ◄

Hodder Murray

A MEMBER OF THE HODDER HEADLINE GROUP

The Publishers would like to thank the following for permission to reproduce copyright material:

**Photo credits**
**p.1, 4, 7** *t*, **8, 9, 19, 23, 59, 61, 62, 72, 73** *l*, **74, 76, 92, 93** and **104** Steve Connolly; **p.7** *c* Yoshikazu Tsuno/AFP/Getty Images; **p.7** *b* LG Electronics UK Ltd; **p.13** Akg-images/British Library; **p.16** *t* © Shout/Alamy; **p.16** *b* © Ian Miles-Flashpoint Pictures/Alamy; **p.21** © Jacques M. Chenet/Corbis; **p.73** *c* © Steve Chenn/Corbis; **p.73** *r* Aristide Economopoulos/The Star-Ledger/Corbis; **p.178** www.purestockX.com.

**Acknowledgements**
**p.17** www.CartoonStock.com; **p.22** www.lancs.ac.uk; **p.29** www.metro.co.uk; **p.32** Definitions from searchmobilecomputing.techtarget.com and searchnetworking.techtarget.com; **p.77** Extract from Tesco company report from The Annual Online Reports Service; **p.99** *l* Play.com *r* National Rail Enquiries; **p.101** *l* Yell.com *r* BT Online; **p.103** Andrew Orlowski, The Register; **pp.104-5** Craig Harris, The Seattle Post-Intelligencer; **p.108** BCS Glossary of ICT and Computing terms.

All AQA material reproduced by permission of the Assessment and Qualifications Alliance.
Every effort has been made to trace all copyright holders, but if any have been inadvertently overlooked the Publishers will be pleased to make the necessary arrangements at the first opportunity.

Although every effort has been made to ensure that website addresses are correct at time of going to press, Hodder Murray cannot be held responsible for the content of any website mentioned in this book. It is sometimes possible to find a relocated web page by typing in the address of the home page for a website in the URL window of your browser.

Hodder Headline's policy is to use papers that are natural, renewable and recyclable products and made from wood grown in sustainable forests. The logging and manufacturing processes are expected to conform to the environmental regulations of the country of origin.

Orders: please contact Bookpoint Ltd, 130 Milton Park, Abingdon, Oxon OX14 4SB.
Telephone: (44) 01235 827720. Fax: (44) 01235 400454. Lines are open 9.00 – 5.00, Monday to Saturday, with a 24-hour message answering service. Visit our website at www.hoddereducation.co.uk

© Barbara Wilson 2007

First published in 2007 by
Hodder Murray, an imprint of Hodder Education,
a member of the Hodder Headline Group,
An Hachette Livre UK Company,
338 Euston Road
London NW1 3BH

Impression number      5  4  3  2  1
Year                                   2012  2011 2010  2009  2008  2007

Cover photo Corbis Images UK, Ltd
Illustrations by Mike Flanagan/Flantoons
Typeset in 11pt Stone Informal by Pantek Arts Ltd.
Printed in Italy

A catalogue record for this title is available from the British Library

ISBN: 978 0340 94011 2

# Contents

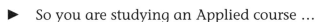

# Introduction

▶ So you are studying an Applied course ...

You may be new to the idea of an applied course, or you may have studied an applied GCSE course or one such as DIDA that has similar characteristics. Applied courses are designed to help you to learn about your subject in a practical rather than a theoretical way.

**Figure 1** Student using a computer

This means that you should be spending lots of time using ICT tools and techniques to produce ICT-based solutions. It doesn't mean that this is all you will have to do and that all of your time will be spent working on a computer; this is because working with ICT is not just about the time you spend at a keyboard. There is also a lot of time that needs to be spent on activities such as design work, talking to other people and just thinking! It does mean though that you will be gaining knowledge and an understanding of the subject in a very practical way.

On this course you will be expected to work with real people and organisations. You will find that you gain a lot more than just facts from getting out and meeting people from different organisations, who are doing different jobs and are using ICT in different ways. There is such a wide variation in what people want ICT to do for them that you should have no difficulty in finding real situations to use and your teacher will be able to help you with this.

## Structure of the course

▶ There are three possible courses that you may be taking, all made up of a combination of units, either 3, 6 or 12 units:

- The single AS award in Applied ICT (3 units)
- The single A level award in Applied ICT (6 units)
- The double A level award in Applied ICT (12 units)

The table on page 2 shows which units you need to take for which award. So that you can mark off which units you are going to be studying, this table is also included as **Item 1** on the CD-ROM enclosed with this book.

**important note**

Externally assessed units are in bold.

| Box 1: AS User units | Box 3: AS Practitioner units |
|---|---|
| Unit 1: ICT and Society<br>Unit 2: ICT and Organisations<br>Unit 3: Data Handling | Unit 4: ICT Solutions<br><br>*Plus any two of*<br>Unit 5: Fundamentals of Programming<br>Unit 6: Computer Artwork<br>Unit 7: Creating a Website |
| **Box 2: A2 User units** | **Box 4: A2 Practitioner units** |
| Unit 8: Project Management<br>**Unit 10: Advanced Spreadsheet**<br>**Design**<br><br>*Plus any one of*<br>Unit 12: Publishing<br>Unit 14: Interactive Multimedia | **Unit 9: Software Development**<br><br>*Plus any two of*<br>Unit 11: Communications and<br>Networks<br>Unit 13: Systems Analysis<br>Unit 15: Supporting ICT Users |

Box 1 = Advanced Subsidiary GCE
Box 1 + Box 2 = Advanced GCE
Box 1 + Box 3 = Advanced Subsidiary GCE (Double Award)
Box 1 + Box 2 + Box 3 + Box 4 = Advanced GCE (Double Award)

As you can see from the table, whichever course you are studying, you have to do Units 1, 2 and 3, so these are the units that are covered by this book. They are known as the **core units** because by studying them you should pick up all of the core knowledge, understanding and skills that you will need. These units form the basis for all of the other units that you may study.

# How this book will help you

▶ No matter which course you study there is certain background information that you need, things to make you think, things to help you produce your work in the right way to get the most marks that you can and certain facts about ways of doing something or developments in ICT that you need to know. You will be able to use this book for reference throughout the course as it will help you with all of these aspects and also give you ideas for where else to go to for extra information to help you when you need it. For example, if you want to find out more about what the examination board has available on their website, go to http://www.aqa.org.uk/qual/gceapplied/ict.

The order in which you study the units doesn't matter; your teacher will decide on that. It may be that you will take all three units at once with a couple of lessons a week on each with different teachers, or you may just have one teacher who spends all their time on one unit at a time. Whichever approach is taken, you will be able to use this book for all of your studies for Units 1 to 3 and once you have read this introduction you can then go to whichever section of the book that you want. You don't need to read it from front to back – just dip in to what you need.

When you have completed the first three units you will find that any other units that you take will follow the same basic pattern. Units 9 and 10 are externally assessed and are similar to Unit 1. All of the other units are similar in structure and assessment to Units 2 and 3. There is more detail on this in the section on portfolios at the end this book.

## The accompanying CD-ROM

The CD-ROM provided with this book gives you extra information and also some exercises to do. Throughout the book, you will find a CD-ROM icon in the margin every time an item on the CD-ROM is referred to. You will be able to use the section menus on the CD-ROM to access each of these items. **Item URLs** on the CD-ROM provides all the web addresses that are referenced in the book.

# Assessment

As you will be carrying out much of your studying in a practical way, the manner in which you will be assessed is practical too. Whether you are doing the single or double award, at AS there is only one unit – Unit 1 – where there is an examination. This is not a traditional 1- or 2-hour written paper but an extended 15 hours of examination time in a computer room when you will have a practical task to carry out. The work from this unit will be externally assessed – marked by a marker appointed by the examination board.

For all of the other units you will be asked to produce a portfolio of evidence to show that you know and understand certain things and that you can put your knowledge into practice by producing ICT-based solutions using different types of software. In other words by **doing**!

The portfolios for Units 2 and 3 will be marked by a teacher in your own centre. The standard of their marking is then checked by the examination board so that everyone who takes the course anywhere in the country has their work marked to the same standard. This is known as **internal assessment**.

These types of assessment require you to be well organised and to manage your time carefully. These are important skills to have. They will help you in all aspects of your future life and are much valued by employers and by higher education as they allow people to be more effective in what they do. You will also find that if you do manage your time better you will get more out of life yourself.

**Figure 2** Different uses of ICT

There are advantages to being assessed in this way because you do not have to worry about sitting an examination. The problem with examinations is that you never know how you are going to feel on the particular day and if you are ill or you panic in the exam room there is really very little you can do about it. With portfolio assessment you always have the choice to improve your work, and to leave doing something to another day – that is, providing you do not leave everything to the last minute!

This book is divided into four sections. Sections 1, 2 and 3 cover each of the three units necessary for the AS single award: Units 1, 2 and 3. For each unit there is information to help you to understand what you have to do for that unit and some tips to help you to gain the best marks that you can. Section 4 gives more general help on how to put together a portfolio so that it clearly shows your ability.

## What will I be assessed on?

All Applied ICT GCE courses set out to assess the same things. You will be assessed against what are known as four **assessment objectives**, or AOs:

■ A01 Practical capability in applying ICT
■ A02 Knowledge and understanding of ICT systems and their roles in organisations and society
■ A03 Application of knowledge, skills and understanding to produce solutions to ICT problems
■ A04 Evaluation of ICT solutions and your own performance

## reminder

Don't forget that AS units are assessed at a 'lower level' of difficulty than A2 units. This means that you should aim to get as many marks as possible in the AS units to help with your overall grade if you are going on to study the course beyond AS.

So what do these mean to you?

Well, the better you understand what someone is looking for the better you are able to show evidence of it! So, for each unit you will find a section that explains what the assessment objectives mean in that unit.

All units will be marked out of 70, but the number of marks for each assessment objective will be different for different units. The only one that stays the same because it is equally important in every unit at AS is A04, which stays on 14 marks.

As all units are marked out of 70, this means that they are all equally important and you will need to do as well as you can on every unit to be sure of getting a good grade overall. It does mean though that if you find one unit particularly difficult, or you don't like working under exam conditions, you can try harder in the other units to make up the marks to what you want.

## Standard ways of working

There are certain things that when working with ICT you have to learn to do so that they become standard to you. They are generally things that people working with ICT have found will improve performance and allow people to work safely. They will also help to ensure the privacy and security of any data that you are using – something that will be really important when you work for someone else rather than just yourself. These include such things as:

- remembering to use sensible file names so you can easily tell what the contents of a file are
- taking breaks from staring at the screen
- deleting unwanted data
- securing data from accidental loss
- transferring data using standard formats
- working with others
- wearing anti-static wristbands.

Some of these are things that you should be doing automatically throughout your work, but exactly what you are required to show evidence of is different for each unit and will be explained in the relevant section of the book.

## Evaluation

You will notice that one of the assessment objectives is about showing that you can evaluate ICT solutions and your own performance. You will learn how to evaluate ICT solutions objectively by comparing what you have produced with what your client required. This is something that you can learn to do quite easily.

What is harder to do successfully is to be able to objectively assess your own performance! None of us likes to be criticised or told we aren't working hard enough or we haven't spent enough time or effort on a piece of work. It is very important though for everyone to be able to do this and it has been included as a requirement in applied courses because employers wanted it to be. They say that people need this skill to be effective in the workplace. They don't mind people who don't spend enough time on testing the first time they do it, but who then realise what they did wrong and put it right the next time. The problem comes with people who think they have done everything right and who never stop to consider what they could have improved on – these people rarely get on in life or work. No one finds self-assessment easy to do. You can probably think of older people you know who are not good at taking criticism or admitting they got something wrong!

You will be expected to review how you have got on with the work in each unit. You are not expected to get everything right first time or to plan your time exactly. Honesty is what is needed when carrying out self-evaluation – admit you didn't spend enough time talking to your client, that you underestimated how long it would take to test your solution, or to get a design drawn up. Pretending you are perfect will definitely not get you better marks!

## TASK 1

**Item 2** on the CD-ROM is a simple self-assessment exercise to give you some ideas on how well you manage your time. It can be found by using the Introduction menu on the CD.

Have a go at answering the questions honestly! Your answers may give you some clues about yourself – your strengths and weaknesses. If you have only just realised that you never plan your work and usually leave it to the last minute, then maybe you could consider creating a time plan for your next piece of work and trying to stick to it. See if you feel happier and perform better because of it. Use your answers to start yourself thinking about how you do things – after all, planning, doing, reflecting and reviewing are skills that employers want all their employees to have.

# What is ICT?

▶ It is important that when you are studying any course in a subject you have a really good understanding of what that subject is about. So here are some things to remember:

- ICT stands for Information and Communications Technology.
- It is concerned with the input, processing, storing, transferring and outputting of information using computer technology.
- There is a difference between studying how to use particular ICT tools, such as a spreadsheet program, and how ICT is used by organisations and society.

A control system is one that we simply give commands to. ICT systems are taken to be those where there is interaction between humans and machines.

This course is concerned with how and why ICT is, and can be, used. It is concerned with ICT systems where the output goes directly to a human being or another ICT system and **not** to control a machine. So we are not concerned with washing machines or toasters – until they start speaking to us and asking for input!

The following table shows some examples of what are and what are not control systems and therefore which systems are acceptable for study on this course.

| Type of system | Control system? ✓ or ✗ | Acceptable for study? ✓ or ✗ | Image | Inputs | Outputs |
|---|---|---|---|---|---|
| Electronic Point of Sale (EPOS) system | ✗ | ✓ | | Prices from stock database; Account details from electronic debit and loyalty cards; Weight of goods from scales. | Electronic funds transfer; Update to stock database leading to replenishment order; Receipt for goods. |
| Electronic wheelchair | ✓ | ✗ | | Signals from sensors fed into computer program. | Object avoidance (wheelchair will follow a wall and navigate through a door opening). |
| Internet-ready refrigerator | ✗ | ✓ | | Fridge reads bar codes on food; Input from touch screen. | Automatic re-ordering of food; Notification when food reaches use-by-date; Recipes from Internet. |
| Central heating controller | ✓ | ✗ | | Input from room sensors and temperature sensor on hot water tank. | Switching boiler on and off. |

**Figure 3** An example of a control system

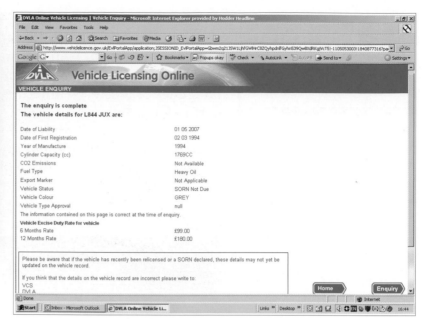

**Figure 4** An example of an ICT system

## TASK 2

**Item 3** on the CD-ROM is an exercise for you to do to show that you understand what is an ICT system and what is a control system.

## Clients

As mentioned already you will be expected to work with real clients, people for whom you will be producing an ICT solution to a problem that they have got. This should not present you with too much difficulty if you think of all of the different people that you see who use ICT each and every day.

Examples could be:

■ a senior manager who needs a report writing on how ICT is being used to help the company maximise profit;
■ a marketing manager who wants a website producing to attract more business;

**Figure 5** Secretary using desktop publishing to create a newsletter

**Figure 6** Graphics designer using ICT

**Figure 7** Accountant working with a spreadsheet on a PC

■ a club secretary who wants a new system for people to apply for membership so that the club can collect data on new members and analyse them to help with future recruitment campaigns.

The senior manager, the marketing manager or the club secretary would be your client.

## Customers or audience

These are the people who will use the solution produced. They may or may not be the same as the client:

■ So for the report they could be the members of the board of directors.
■ For the website they could be the general public.
■ For the membership system they could be cricket players and supporters between 15 and 60 years of age.

For every solution that you produce, you will need to be clear about who the client is and who the users and/or customers are. That is why for Unit 1 you are set a task by the examination board that tells you whom your solution is for.

### reminder

1. 'Applied' means the course involves doing things.
2. You need to find out what actually goes on in real life.
3. You need to be clear what ICT is.
4. You need to be clear what you will be assessed on.
5. You need to be clear how you will be assessed.

### TASK 3

**Item 4** on the CD-ROM is an exercise for you to complete to make sure that you understand what is meant by clients and customers/users for different ICT systems. You need to be sure that you understand the different terms because they are used throughout the specification for this course.

You will find more about this in each section of the book.

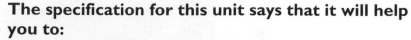

# ICT and society

**The specification for this unit says that it will help you to:**

▶ understand how developments in technology have influenced individuals and society
▶ communicate and present information which is well suited to its purpose and audience.

## Assessment for this unit

▶ This is the only unit at AS that is externally assessed. You will have to complete an assignment set by the examination board under examination conditions in a computer room and you will have to spend investigation time preparing what you will need for these controlled conditions.

You will be assessed against the four assessment objectives:

■ AO1 Practical capability in applying ICT
■ AO2 Knowledge and understanding of ICT systems and their roles in organisations and society
■ AO3 Application of knowledge, skills and understanding to produce solutions to ICT problems
■ AO4 Evaluation of ICT solutions and your own performance

## Background knowledge needed

▶ In all the units there is a certain amount of background knowledge and understanding that you need to gain before starting to carry out the work that is assessed. This may be taught to you, you may be given different exercises to do or you might carry out individual research activities. This section of the book helps to show what it is you need to know and understand and gives you the key facts, but there are also references to other activities to carry out and research sources to look at because the content of this book alone will not be sufficient for you to do well in this unit.

## TASK 1

For the external assessment in this unit you will have to undertake research using the Internet, written sources and other sources of information. You will also need to record where you got your information from and how reliable you consider it to be.

On the CD-ROM there are two items:

- **Item 5** – guidance on bibliographies: what to include and some questions to ask to test the reliability of information sources.
- **Item 6** – a sample bibliography: this is laid out as requested by the exam board for the June 2006 examination.

Your teacher will have given you some information about the course that you are following. Now do a search for information on AQA's GCE Applied ICT course. Use different sources and types of information and record all of your sources in a bibliography.

---

### reminder

**Item URLs** on the CD-ROM has a list of all of the web addresses referenced in this book.

---

ICT is something that has revolutionised the way in which individuals and organisations carry out the activities involved in everyday life – work, leisure, travel and so on. As a result, society as a whole has changed and it is really important that you understand not only the impact that using ICT has, and will have, on you as an individual, but also how it is shaping the society in which you live.

It is important that you can be objective in the way that you look at the ICT technology that is available. Not every development is a good thing for society – there are nearly always both benefits and disadvantages. Take email, for example, which is wonderful for keeping in touch quickly and easily worldwide, but is also a new means to spread viruses, to con individuals out of money and to stalk people!

---

### reminder

Make sure that you know what an Internet search engine is and the names of several different search engines that you can use.

Make sure you know the answers to these questions:

- What is Google?
- What does 'to Google' mean?
- What are given as the results of a query to a search engine?

---

## TASK 2

Think of examples that you know of that show how using email:

- can give benefits to individuals and/or society
- can cause problems for individuals and/or society.

Think of your own experiences with email, look for articles in newspapers and magazines and try Internet searches. One of the disadvantages is the lack of face-to-face communication. Check out this address:
http://counsellingresource.com/counselling-service/online-disadvantages.html
to see the disadvantages of counselling by email.

You will have grown up with ICT being used around you and using it yourself in many different ways, but frequently just for your own benefit. This unit requires you to think from a wider perspective:

- to see other people's views of developments, including:
  - those of younger and older people
  - people from different environments and localities
  - people with different levels of familiarity with ICT
- to appreciate the impact of ICT in different areas of life
- to understand the differences that occur in different geographical areas:
  - rural/urban
  - UK/Europe
  - around the world.

The tasks that are set by the examination board encourage a wider understanding to be demonstrated and you are given a target audience for the newsletter or web pages that you have to produce. This means that you need to be able to understand which aspects of ICT are or aren't important for different groups of people.

## TASK 3

Think of several different uses of ICT that have benefits for society and several that have disadvantages. Try to also think of something where there is a benefit for individuals but disadvantages for society as a whole. **Item 7** on the CD-ROM provides a table for you to use to fill in your examples.

## So what are the changes ICT has brought to society?

Remember what ICT is about and you can see that basically it allows individuals and organisations to:

- input data
- process data
- store data
- transfer data
- output information.

These are things that people have been doing for hundreds of years. But what makes the way we do these activities different today using ICT is the fact that we can now do them more quickly, over longer distances and in greater volumes than we ever could before. This increases the quality and quantity of the information we can obtain. This in turn affects what we can do with that information and the knowledge we can obtain from it.

Obtaining and using information has always been a key to success and power. In June 1815 Europe was in turmoil, with Napoleon's armies having conquered much of Europe. There was rising panic in Britain that Napoleon would defeat the new British army that had been sent to Belgium and the stock market fell as a result. The Rothschild family, a well-known family of financiers, had built up an intelligence network unrivalled anywhere in Europe. They were kept informed of Napoleon's activities, often weeks in advance of the government, by using a large flock of carrier pigeons to carry the information. So they knew, well in advance of anyone else, that The Duke of Wellington had defeated Napoleon at the Battle of Waterloo. This was so contrary to expectation that they were able to use this information to buy up shares at rock bottom prices. As a result, they already owned large quantities of shares when the news of the victory 'officially' arrived. The good news caused the price of shares to soar and the Rothschild fortune to increase by a reputed 20 times.

In the same way, today, organisations are still looking for ways to be the first to learn key information, in order to be able to use it to their best advantage. The difference is that now ICT is used to gather and transmit the information rather than carrier pigeons.

**Figure 1.1** Wellington at the Battle of Waterloo

**definition**

**Data**
Data are raw facts and figures, or sets of values, measurements or records of transactions. They have no meaning and have not been processed.

For example, the numbers that make up a bar code or the values for each pixel in a photograph.

**Information**
Information is data that have been processed or converted by an ICT system to give them meaning, to organise them or give them a context.

For example, the description of a product and its price found by the software processing the bar code, or a scanned image made up from the pixel values.

**Knowledge**
Knowledge is a set of rules or concepts used to interpret or 'make sense of' information.

For example, a sales manager is able to interpret the monthly sales figures in a report produced for them by the sales order processing system to decide whether sales are increasing as a result of a new marketing campaign.

## What is an information system?

A system that produces information in any form that can be understood by humans – words, sounds, still or moving pictures – is known as an **information system**. Obviously not all information that is produced by information systems is good information and it is important to understand what makes information of good quality so that we can ensure that when we produce ICT solutions they do what they are supposed to do and produce good quality information for the people who use them. It will be important in this unit that you start to look at different newsletters and web pages critically so that you can gain a better understanding of how different people look at information and that what is good for one person may not be for another. This will help you in your assignment when you have to 'research the needs of the audience' (see pages 37–9).

## Good information

The characteristics of good information are different for different people. What is up to date for one person may not be for another. For example, someone ordering a jumper from an Internet store needs to know the price of the jumper at the time they order it, not how much it cost last week or next week. The sales staff of the Internet store will need to know what the price was that they charged for the jumper when it was sold – this might be a week after the sale took place but is still up to date for their purpose.

Only an information system that produces the information that people want in the form that they want it in will be successful.

## TASK 4

When you are doing your investigation work for the assessment in this unit you will need to find out exactly what information your target audience wants and in what form, so that you can produce good information for the client. So try asking people of different ages and backgrounds what they like best and why:

- Pictures or words?
- Graphs or numbers?
- Text that is split up by pictures or blocks of text and separate pictures?
- Brightly coloured or in paler shades?
- Large or small fonts, in different font styles or the same font style?
- What do they consider to be reliable?
- What do they consider to be up to date and accurate?

 **Item 22** on the CD-ROM provides some useful tips on how you can find out exactly what information the target audience wants.

## case study 2
### ▶ Successful – the DVLA database

The DirectGov website has a section where you can search for vehicle details – useful if you want to buy a genuine car. This interface to the DVLA database is simple and the details are accurate. Some information systems are less successful.

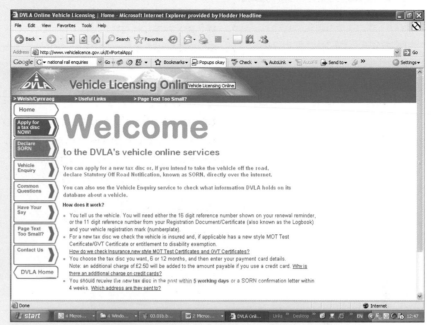

**Figure 1.2** The DVLA home page

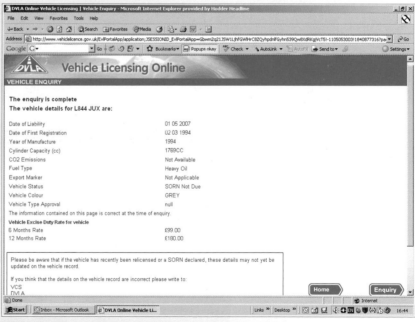

**Figure 1.3** Page showing results of a vehicle enquiry

## case study 3
▶ Unsuccessful – The London Ambulance Service

In October 1992 the London Ambulance Service implemented a new system. Designed to speed up the dispatch of ambulances, it quickly ground to a halt because it presented the operators with:

- information that disappeared off the screens before they could read it
- information that was duplicated
- incorrect information about the location of ambulances.

The result was chaos and the operators had to revert to a fully manual system. News stories at the time claimed that several people lost their lives as a result.

**Figure 1.4** An ambulance control room

**Figure 1.5** Ambulance en route to an emergency

## TASK 5

Can you find other examples of successful and unsuccessful ICT systems? Try searching for news stories. You will probably find more about the unsuccessful ones! Why is this?

## Changes in ICT and their effects on society

Knowing a little bit about how ICT has evolved over the years helps us to understand what is happening now and also how ICT may be used in the future.

### In the beginning ...

Initially, computer systems were used as large calculators to deal with huge quantities of very simple calculations for banks and building societies, electricity and gas companies and local councils, for example. Only small quantities of data were stored in these systems; they were used to produce bills and statements. Some of the earliest effects of ICT on society were the excuses made for incorrect bills such as 'the computer has made a mistake'. This of course led people to believe that computers were very clever and that they had a mind of their own!

"Wait guys, It was all a computer error"

**Figure 1.6** www.CartoonStock.com

Of course this is something which is impossible because any computer system will only do what it has been instructed to do – either the person who wrote the programs instructing the computer or the person using the program or entering data got it wrong, not the computer.

Improvements in devices for storing data enabled organisations to start storing more data. Developments in programming languages such as the third generation language COBOL meant that it became easier for organisations to start sorting and searching large quantities of data to obtain the information that they required to run their businesses and enable them to start offering different services to customers.

## Data protection

At this point concern started to be raised about the volume of data on individuals that was being stored electronically and legislation was introduced to try to protect the individual. This was when the first Data Protection Act was introduced.

### reminder

**PRINCIPLES OF THE DATA PROTECTION ACT**

The data protection principles say that data must be:

1. fairly and lawfully processed
2. processed for registered purposes
3. adequate, relevant and not excessive
4. accurate and up to date
5. not kept for longer than is necessary
6. processed in line with your rights
7. secure
8. not transferred to countries without adequate protection.

To find out more, go to:
http://www.ico.gov.uk/ what_we_cover/ data_protection/ the_basics.aspx

### TASK 6

Ask some different people of different ages if they have heard of Data Protection legislation and if they know what it means for them personally.

One of the biggest problems with the Data Protection legislation is that it is up to organisations to declare what data they are storing. This means that you only know about the data stored by organisations who have registered with the Information Commissioner and are on the register; you don't know about the ones that aren't. Also, you can't find out about organisations that haven't declared all of the data that they store.

### TASK 7

The web page http://www.ico.gov.uk/tools_and_resources.aspx gives you a selection of information from the Information Commissioner's office. One of the links on this page takes you to the register of data controllers. Look up some organisations that you know, for example, your school or college, your bank or building society or other local organisations. See what data they store and for what purpose.

Here is an example of what you might see if you searched for a sports club.

Note that there are a lot of other useful links and pieces of information on this website that you might be able to use for your work.

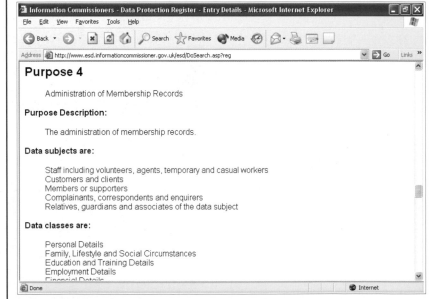

**Figure 1.7** Results of search for a sports club

## Banking

In banking, the introduction of Automated Teller Machines (ATMs) transformed the way in which we carry out some of our banking transactions. Originally these just allowed people to take out cash because the machines were not online to the main data stores. This meant the ATMs could not provide details of your current bank balance (how much money you have or haven't got). Also, to begin with, you could only use the cash machine owned by the bank that you had your account with. However, once the banks got together and introduced reciprocal systems you could then use other banks' machines. Improvements in technology, particularly the use of magnetic stripe cards and improved communication techniques, made it possible to introduce these systems; this was really when the 'C' came into ICT!

## TASK 8

Answer the following questions about cash machines:

1 Where are they situated and why?
2 What are the benefits to the banks' customers?
3 What are the disadvantages for the banks' customers?
4 What can you do at one today?
5 What does 'online' mean?
6 What is used now instead of magnetic strips and why?
7 Can you use any cash machine anywhere?

See also **Item 8** on the CD-ROM.

**Figure 1.8** ATM on a high street

## Retailing

The use of ICT systems by large retail chains and supermarkets to provide quick processing of sales by introducing automated tills and then stock control systems, was something which started to affect society. These systems became more complex, with the addition of systems for loyalty cards, EFTPOS cards and store cards. Today, online shopping using the Internet is becoming more and more common, but this has problems associated with it as well as benefits. As mentioned earlier, ICT doesn't allow us to do anything new; it just lets us do things in a different way. Internet shopping has replaced the process of telephoning an order to a shop and having it delivered or, further back in time, of sending the servants down to the local grocers with a list!

### definition

**EFTPOS**

EFTPOS – Electronic Funds Transfer at Point of Sale. EFTPOS is a system that is used to take funds directly from your bank account or credit card account when you use a compatible card to pay for goods.

### case study 4
▶ Amazon

In July 1995, Amazon.com sold its first book. Over the 2005 Christmas season, Amazon sold a staggering 108 million items. It made its first profit, just $5 million, at the end of 2002, but made $8.5 billion profit in 2005. In ten years it had become one of the top 500 companies in the United States. Amazon's aim is to sell everything that anyone might want, in one place.

### case study 5
▶ Tesco

Tesco launched its store-based home shopping service, Tesco.com, in 1999. Allowing its customers to shop from home and have the goods delivered to them has been a huge success. The service had a turnover of £700 million in 2004/2005, making it the largest Internet grocery in the world. The service covers 96% of UK households.

*Source:* http://www.tescocorporate.com/publiclibs/tesco/retailingservices.pdf

### TASK 9

Discuss the impact that Tesco's home delivery service has had on its customers. If 96% of UK households are covered geographically, are there any of these that are unlikely to use it? If so, what might be the reason for this?

## TASK 10

**Item 9** on the CD-ROM contains a list of questions that you could use to interview people about developments that have taken place in retailing. This will enable you to discover just what people think about these developments. For example, are they what everyone wants or do older people not like what is happening?

### Personal Communications

Once manufacturing companies had the technology available to produce personal computers at an acceptable cost, personal computing 'took off'. Soon many homes began to purchase these new machines, although initially many were only used for word processing, and in fact early versions were just that; word processing machines.

**Figure 1.9** An early personal computer

Small businesses could now afford to have computers and so it became much more common to receive standard letters and invoices produced on these systems. The advent of personal computing also brought with it threats from viruses, as personal users started trying to 'hack' into organisations' systems. Again, it became necessary to introduce legislation to combat these threats and the Computer Misuse Act was introduced.

**case study 6**
▶ **The importance of the Computer Misuse Act**

Students often overlook the importance of the Act. To help you put it into context, here is an extract from the website of Lancaster University outlining some examples of how they see students contravening the act!

■ **Example 1, Unauthorised Access to Computer Material.**
*This would include: using another person's identifier (ID) and password without proper authority in order to use data or a program, or to alter, delete, copy or move a program or data, or simply to output a program or data (for example, to a screen or printer); laying a trap to obtain a password; reading examination papers or examination results.*

*The response to some actions will depend on the specific conditions of use in force. Take, for example, unauthorised borrowing of an identifier from another student in order to obtain more time for a computer project the student was required to complete. In this case both the student who borrowed the ID and the student who lent it would be deemed to have committed an offence.*

■ **Example 2, Unauthorised Access to a Computer with intent.**
*This would include: gaining access to financial or administrative records, but intent would have to be proved.*

■ **Example 3, Unauthorised Modification of Computer Material.**
*This would include: destroying another user's files; modifying system files; creation of a virus; introduction of a local virus; introduction of a networked virus; changing examination results; and deliberately generating information to cause a complete system malfunction.*

*Universities and Colleges should recognise that action under disciplinary procedures is more effective if a similar view is taken across the sector and if institutions are prepared to discipline their students for offences carried out across the network on the facilities of other universities and colleges. It is desirable that as far as possible similar offences in different institutions carry similar penalties.*

*Source:* http://www.lancs.ac.uk/iss/rules/cmisuse.htm

## TASK 11

Find out what the penalties are for contravening the Computer Misuse Act in your school or college. Are they different for staff and students? Should they be?

## IT becomes 'user friendly'

The development of 'user friendly' operating systems and interfaces, such as those on Apple machines and the Microsoft Windows environment, and more recently Microsoft Vista, made the technology more accessible to a wider range of people. These interfaces were supposed to be more intuitive for people to use and did not rely on people remembering commands. Instead, commands are provided via the use of icons and menus, and navigation and selection is done using mice or pointers instead of keys. These are called WIMP environments.

---

**definition**

**WIMP**
WIMP – Windows, Icons, Menus and Pointers.

---

**Figure 1.10** The DOS prompt

**Figure 1.12** Microsoft Windows XP

**Figure 1.11** Apple Mac user interface

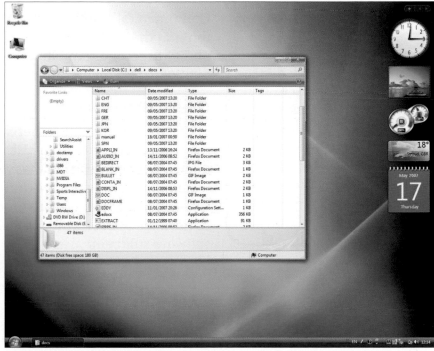

**Figure 1.13** iPod full-screen menu interface

**Figure 1.14** Microsoft Windows Vista

Users come in all shapes and sizes and their needs are different. The interface that is suitable for a data input clerk using a system all day every day will be quite different from one provided for someone using an ICT system on the only occasion they visit a tourist attraction.

For this unit you need to know what are good and bad interfaces for different groups of people. This may be an issue that you want to include information on in your newsletter or web pages. You may want to investigate the different types of hand-held devices available, the different interfaces used on mobile phones, or interfaces adapted for people with particular needs.

## TASK 12

1   Write down five things you like about the Windows® interface and five things that you don't like.
2   Compare your list with some other people.
3   Are the things you like the same or are they different? Why?

**Item 10** on the CD-ROM gives a list of rules that could be used when designing interfaces.

1   How well does the Windows® environment follow these?
2   List what would be needed to make an interface 'friendly' to a person with a sight disability.
3   Would the list be different if the person had an upper limb disability instead?

Continued falls in the cost of equipment and software keep making the number of computers in existence rise and the ability to recondition old ones has helped to make them available to a greater number of people worldwide.

### Global differences

There are considerable differences in how easily people around the world, and even in the UK, can access technology. There is a tendency to think that everyone has access to the sort of technology that you have and many students can get a surprise when they go into organisations and discover the lack of hardware or software, or what they consider to be old software still being used!

## TASK 13

1 Can you discover how many homes actually own a computer:
   a  in the UK?
   b  worldwide?
2 Are there differences between individual countries?
3 If people haven't got their own computer in your area, where can they go to use one?
4 How available is broadband technology:
   a  in the UK?
   b  in other parts of the world?
5 Is there a difference between the availability of broadband in rural areas and urban areas?
6 Does the availability of broadband have an effect on the uses made of ICT?

**case study 7**
**► The digital divide**

The digital divide is seen as a technological divide between developed and developing countries. But there is also a divide within developed countries between those who have access to ICT and those who do not. The following article on the digital divide leads to some interesting figures on Internet access and PC ownership:
http://www.caslon.com.au/dividesprofile.htm

According to the figures shown, Greece has only nine PCs per 100 head of population whereas Estonia has 87!

## TASK 14

Carry out a simple survey to find out what percentage of people in your area has access to a computer at home. Make sure that you ask people from a broad spectrum of age groups.

■ Are your results representative of the country as a whole?
■ How do you think your results compare with other countries?

## Reconditioning and disposal – old computers never die!

As more and more computers come into existence every time someone buys a new one, what happens to the old ones?

## TASK 15

Answer the following questions:
1 How can you get rid of an unwanted computer?
2 Could you give your computer to a less economically developed country?
3 Are there any risks associated with disposing of old computers?
4 What would you do with the data on your hard disk before getting rid of your computer?

There are a number of charities that recondition old computers and send them to developing countries. Many of these charities are reputable and provide much needed resources for the developing world. But how safe is it to do this to your computer? The BBC One programme 'Real Story', 14 August 2006, told the story of Ted Roberts, from Essex, whose personal details were found on a computer hard drive bought by a BBC reporter for £15 in a market in Nigeria. The full story can be found at:

http://news.bbc.co.uk/1/hi/programmes/real_story/4791167.stm

What are the benefits and pitfalls of 'recycling' computers in this way, both to the donors and the recipients?

## Changes in the technology available

As you can see from some of the earlier examples, changes in the available technology trigger different uses to which ICT can be put. This applies not just to developments in the hardware, but developments in the software as well. The development of relational database technology meant a change in the way many businesses could operate; suddenly they could store information more efficiently and relate this information together. In banking, for example, all of a customer's accounts and personal details could be related along with details of any mortgages or insurance policies so that the bank could change to customer-based, rather than account-based, marketing. Personal banking took off as a result. Customers noticed a change in the way their bank statements were provided and in how they did business with the banks.

ANY BANK

L B Smith
187 Park Road
Cumbria

ACCOUNT NUMBER: 10045321
SORT CODE: 90-99-19

STATEMENT: 17
NUMBER:
PAGE: 1 of 1

**TRANSACTION DETAILS**

| DATE | DESCRIPTION | | DEBITS | CREDITS | BALANCE | |
|------|-------------|---|--------|---------|---------|---|
| Balance brought forward | | | | | 35 | 00 |
| 6 May | CD07 | High St | 10 00 | | 25 | 00 |
| 8 May | DC07 | Pet Care Plc | 3 00 | | 22 | 00 |
| 11 May | BACS | Regular Times | | 46 50 | 68 | 50 |
| 19 May | CH007 | | 2 70 | | 65 | 80 |
| 19 May | DD | Gas & Co | 16 50 | | 49 | 30 |
| 22 May | S0 | TV Licence Company | 21 00 | | 28 | 30 |

**Figure 1.15** Example of a bank statement before ICT was used

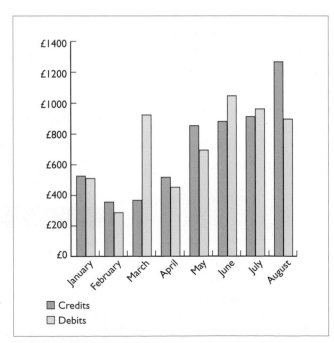

▣ Credits
▢ Debits

**Figure 1.16** Example of a financial summary from a recent bank statement

## The Internet

Few developments in ICT have changed so many different aspects of society as the Internet, and yet so little is understood about it! Its development has been so rapid and its usage is increasing all the time. So what is it?

---

## What is the Internet?

■ The Internet is an infrastructure (like a road system) for data to be moved over.
  NB It is always moved as data, but presented as information when viewed.
■ It is a series of nodes (usually computers) connected together by cables and radio links.
■ Routers are used to send data along suitable routes between the nodes.
■ It is not owned by anyone.
■ Standards have been agreed for addressing and for the transfer of data.

Have a look at the websites listed below to find out more about the story and standards associated with the Internet and the World Wide Web:
http://www.isoc.org/internet/standards/
http://www.w3.org/Consortium/
For discussions on who controls the Internet, visit:
http://www.foreignaffairs.org/20051101facomment 84602-p0/ kenneth-neil-cukier/who-will-control-the-internet.html
http://technology.guardian.co.uk/weekly/story/ 0,16376,1585288,00.html

---

### reminder

In your work for this unit you are asked to reference all the sources of information you use (this means all sources, not just Internet-based ones) and how you have ensured that the information that you have used is valid.

Imagine if you were working for a company and were asked to research the cost of replacement ink cartridges. You get a price and the company orders them only to discover that the price you provided them with was two years out of date and the order has now cost them a lot more!

### Uses of the Internet

The Internet has allowed people almost instant access to vast amounts of information held in many different places worldwide over the World Wide Web. It has also enabled organisations to make use of the infrastructure to offer goods and services to people in ways that were not previously possible, for example, online banking and shopping, applications for official documents like driving licences, insurance quotes, medical services, travel information and flight bookings; the list is endless. Phrases like e-commerce, e-shopping, e-booking and e-banking are now commonly used.

One very important consideration that you need to be aware of when using the Internet is the reliability of the information that is available over the Internet. This is why it is so important that you are able to make sensible choices as to what you believe or don't believe from the information that you find there.

The use of webcams and podcasts brings a new meaning to the phrase 'big brother is watching you' and the speed at which news can travel across the Internet has far-reaching consequences for everyone, especially when it has political implications. Politicians in some countries have been worried about the access to information about other cultures that the Internet provides.

### TASK 16

Try searching for information from newspapers, such as on the technology Guardian website (http://technology.guardian.co.uk), for news on China and its Internet police. The following websites are also of interest:

- For the start of the story concerning Google's filtered Chinese service, visit:
  http://news.com.com/No+booze+or+jokes+for+Googlers+in+China/2100-1030_3-6031727.html
- For censorship of the Internet in Singapore, visit:
  http://news.com.com/2100-1023-217236.html
- A different perspective on China's Internet Police can be found in the article 'A Day In The Life Of A Chinese Internet Police Officer' at:
  http://www.zonaeuropa.com/20060208_1.htm

 Remember these links are also provided in **Item URLs** on the CD-ROM.

## Consequences of using ICT

Often, ICT is used to enable something without full consideration being given to the consequences. One example is video clips of wartime activities that can be viewed virtually live. This means that people can see their relatives in action or worse still, being killed. Another example is the increase in incorrect medical self-diagnosis that is going on – people imagine they have illnesses that they haven't got because they have been looking at the symptoms on an online medical service or are buying sub-standard drugs online and not receiving the treatment that they should.

For a discussion of the value of general practitioners using Google for online diagnoses, go to:
http://www.metro.co.uk/news/article.html?in_article_id=24627&in_page_id=34.

### How the Internet is used to obtain information

Initially the Internet was used primarily for displaying information for people to read, but more recently there has been a growing trend for it to be used for obtaining information from readers as well. For example, online surveys are now conducted by many market research organisations, and companies have introduced their own surveys in the form of questions that they ask when you purchase something from their websites.

For more information on this, visit:

■ customer satisfaction surveys at Companies House:
http://www.companieshouse.gov.uk/about/custSatSurvey.shtml

■ the DVLA website:
http://www.dvla.gov.uk

■ a site that specialises in online market research:
http://www.brainjuicer.com/.

## case study 9
### ► Doctors and the Internet

Doctors are being urged to use Google searches to help them diagnose illnesses.

They can come up with a correct diagnosis in seconds, just by typing in a patient's symptoms, a study showed. Search engines were becoming vital tools in clinical medicine and 'doctors in training need to become proficient in their use', the researchers added.

However, their findings provoked concerns that doctors could make deadly mistakes by taking information from unverified sources. The Patients Association said: 'I would have thought that doctors would feel qualified enough to make a diagnosis without accessing the Web.'

Searching for health information is one of the most common uses of the Web and Google has more than 3 billion medical articles.

The researchers Googled the symptoms of 26 conditions, including the hormonal disorder Cushing's syndrome and CJD, the human form of mad cow disease.

The findings were correct in 58 per cent of cases.

Australian researchers Hangwi Tang and Jennifer Hwee Kwoo wrote in the British Medical Journal: 'Useful information on even the rarest medical syndromes can now be found and digested within a matter of minutes.'

Their interest was piqued when they heard that a doctor successfully diagnosed an immune system disorder, called Ipex Syndrome, online.

Other studies have shown doctors misdiagnose fatal illnesses in one in five cases.

However, the craze for patients self-diagnosing on the Web has led to the rise of 'cyberchondriacs' who rely on inaccurate online information.

Prof Mayur Lakhani, of the Royal College of General Practitioners said: 'The Net is not a replacement for going to see a doctor or nurse for a diagnosis.'

*Source*: http://www.metro.co.uk/news/article.html?in_article_id=24627&in_page_id=34

## Problems associated with Internet usage

Like many developments in ICT, use of the Internet comes at a cost. There are problems associated with it as well as the many benefits it provides.

### TASK 17

Using the information provided in **Item 11** on the CD-ROM, do your own research into how the Internet has affected different areas of life:

- Education
- Travel
- Banking and insurance
- Health
- Sport
- Leisure
- Personal communications

Look out for the advantages and disadvantages of using the Internet for each area and whether the effects are greatest for certain types or ages of people or in particular areas of the country or world. Also think about whether people treat information found or given over the Internet differently to that found in books or newspapers or given in a personal interview.

## Connections and devices

Changes in the technology available apply to devices and communication techniques as well as computers. Today there is a wider choice of ways of connecting devices than ever before, making use of the ability to send data down different media and making the idea of a PAN an actuality! Imagine a plane containing a group of passengers all connected to their

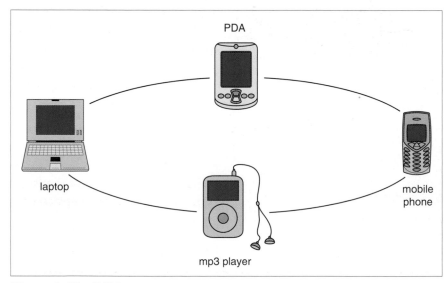

**Figure 1.17a** PAN

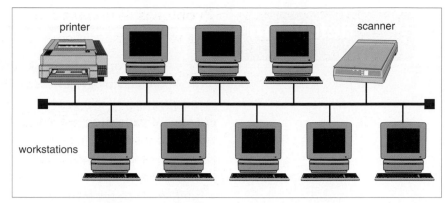

**Figure 1.17b** LAN

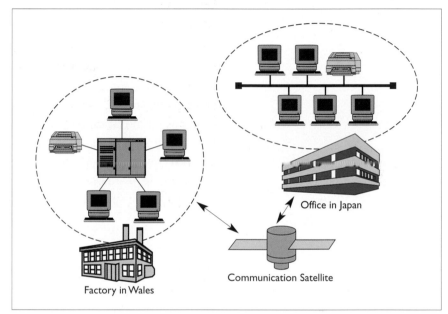

**Figure 1.17c** WAN

own individual networks, to the LAN within the plane, through that to the Internet and through the Internet to WANs for their own organisations! One of the biggest problems with anything to do with networks is in being able to visualise the idea of data moving through time and space at vast speeds in lots of different directions.

## definition

### PAN

PAN – A personal area network (PAN) is the interconnection of information technology devices within the range of an individual person, typically within a range of 10 metres. For example, a person travelling with a laptop, a personal digital assistant (PDA), and a portable printer could interconnect these devices without having to plug anything in, using some form of wireless technology. Typically, this kind of personal area network could also be interconnected without wires to the Internet or other networks.

*Source*: http://searchmobilecomputing.techtarget.com/sDefinition/ 0,,sid40_gci546288,00.html

### LAN

LAN – A local area network (LAN) is a group of computers and associated devices that share a common communications line or wireless link. Typically, connected devices share the resources of a single processor or server within a small geographic area (for example, within an office building). Usually, the server has applications and data storage that are shared in common by multiple computer users. A local area network may serve as few as two or three users (for example, in a home network) or as many as thousands of users (for example, in an FDDI network).

*Source*: http://searchnetworking.techtarget.com/sDefinition/0,,sid7_gci212495,00.html

### WAN

WAN – A wide area network (WAN) is a geographically dispersed telecommunications network. The term distinguishes a broader telecommunications structure from a local area network (LAN). A wide area network may be privately owned or rented, but the term usually connotes the inclusion of public (shared user) networks. An intermediate form of network in terms of geography is a metropolitan area network (MAN).

*Source*: http://searchnetworking.techtarget.com/sDefinition/ 0,290660,sid7_gci214117,00.html

# Software skills

▶ At the same time as you are increasing your knowledge and understanding of how in general the use of ICT has affected society, you will need to ensure that you have the necessary skills in the use of the software package you will be using to produce your newsletter or web pages.

If you look at a mark scheme for one of the past assignments (see **Item 13** and **Item 14** on the CD-ROM) you will see that to achieve the higher marks for A01 on practical skills and also for A03 you need to not only be able to use features of the software package, but also to understand and explain why you are using a particular feature and how it is suitable for the work that you are doing. A skilled ICT worker who produces good solutions understands when it is appropriate to use a feature, such as applying bullets or watermarking pages, and doesn't just include it because they know how, to show off their skills.

The specification contains a list of the sort of features you might be using to produce good information. The AQA website can be accessed at: http://www.aqa.org.uk/qual/, where you can view the specification that is relevant to your year of study. Remember you are studying an **Applied** GCE A/AS subject.

One of the important things that you must learn to do is to set up your own templates. Most software packages of the sort that you will be using provide standard templates for different types of documents or different web page layouts. As someone following an ICT specialist course, you should be able to create your own templates to use. This is something you are likely to find very useful in the future as templates save time! Do not simply use a standard template for your newsletter because you will not be able to gain good marks if you do. The emphasis is on you producing something that is suitable for a particular purpose and a particular audience.

# The assignment

▶ To get an idea of exactly how you are going to be assessed in this unit and what you will need to do, have a look at any past assignments and mark schemes that you can find on the examination board website:
http://www.aqa.org.uk/qual/gceapplied/ict-assess.php.

The task for June 2006 is included as **Item 13** on the CD-ROM. An example of an assignment might be something like:

> You have been asked to produce a set of eight web pages for inclusion on a website run by a local community group, such as the local cricket club. The web pages should contain information about:
>
> Three examples of ways members of the group could make use of the Internet, one of which must be appropriate for a group of people with particular needs; two examples of problems with using the Internet for members of the group; one example of legislation that would affect the community group's use of ICT.

## important note

This list is taken from the Candidate Booklets that are issued by the examination board on either 1 November (if you are submitting your work in January the following year) or 1 April (if you are submitting your work in June). This list will stay more or less the same but you **must** read the instructions that you receive carefully so that you are aware of any differences in the list below.

Look at the Candidate Booklet on the CD-ROM – **Item 13**. You will notice that the time that you have available for the assignment is divided into two periods:

- Investigation time
- Controlled conditions

The investigation time can be as long as you want after the publication of the assignment. Your teacher will advise you on how long you will have available. The amount of time for the controlled conditions, which are examination conditions held in a computer room, is fixed at 15 hours for this unit. This means that all of the items that have to be produced during controlled conditions must be done under these conditions **and** must be completed during the 15 hours.

The following is a list of all of the items that you will have to produce and include in the work handed in, as evidence to show your knowledge, skills and understanding for this unit.

To be completed during the investigation time:
- ▶ A plan for the work to be done showing what needs to be carried out, the sequence of activities and the time involved for all of the work (investigation time and controlled conditions).
- ▶ Evidence of an understanding of the needs of the audience for which the newsletter/web pages are intended, from which the assessment criteria for evaluation are derived.
- ▶ The evaluation criteria for the newsletter/web pages to assess its suitability for purpose and audience.
- ▶ Evidence of testing the draft designs of the newsletter/web pages and any steps taken to correct errors and/or make other changes to try to ensure that the needs of the audience have been met.
- ▶ Final design for the format and structure of the newsletter/web pages to show evidence of their planning.
- ▶ A detailed bibliography listing the sources used while researching and gathering the material to be used for the newsletter/web pages.
- ▶ Listing of files containing pre-prepared research material to be used during controlled conditions.

To be produced during the controlled conditions:

- ▶ Screenshots to show how the newsletter/web pages was/were composed and developed, cross-referenced to the research files.
- ▶ A printout of the completed newsletter/web pages.
- ▶ An annotated printout of the template used for the newsletter/web pages displaying the range of features of the software that were used.
- ▶ A list of all the files used, annotated to show amendments and additions to the initial list.
- ▶ An evaluation of the newsletter/web pages produced, using evidence from testing to show that the audience needs and the evaluation criteria have, or have not, been met.
- ▶ A record to show whether the time plan was followed and any adjustments made in order to complete the tasks.

▶

▶ An evaluation of the candidate's own performance in completing the work and following their plan.

▶ Evidence that they have followed standard ways of working in completing this assignment, particularly in terms of managing their work and keeping it secure.

Also:

▶ Evidence of appropriate written communication throughout the work.

## Investigation time

### Planning

Once you have a copy of the assignment and know from your teacher how much investigation time you have and when your 15 hours of controlled conditions will be, the first thing to do is to make a plan of how you are going to spend your time. Figure 1.18 gives an idea of part of a plan used by one student for the investigation time. You will notice that this student has included their reasons for certain dates or times being set. This, along with what the student writes in the final column, will help that student with their planning for future units that they have to do. This is because it will alert them to where their plan went wrong so that they can avoid making the same mistake in the future!

You may find it easier to divide up your investigation time into week blocks and the time for the controlled conditions into the different sessions that you will have.

The requirements are for you to produce the following:

■ A plan for the work to be done, showing what needs to be carried out, the sequence of activities and the time involved for all of the work (investigation time and controlled conditions).
■ A record to show whether this plan was followed and any adjustments made in order to complete the tasks.

When you are planning your work, make sure that you have a clear understanding of what you have got to do in the available time. You need to make sure that you leave sufficient time for things to perhaps not go quite as you imagine they will. Leaving a little spare time at the end of the investigation time would be sensible, just in case you have any problems.

The record should show where you got behind or in front of your time plan, and how you adjusted it to take account of delays or how you spent the extra time you found you had. Be honest – the examiners are looking to see whether you have learnt from what you have done. For example, many students often underestimate how long it takes to find the images that they need or to complete the detailed design work that they require for the controlled conditions.

This is a rough draft that should be word processed during the investigation time and taken into the controlled conditions as a paper copy to complete as the controlled sessions are taken. Word processing at all in controlled conditions will waste your time.

| Task | Start date | Complete by | Comments/Reasons | Finished on time or not and why |
|---|---|---|---|---|
| Investigate styles of presenting information for the specified audience | 1/11/06 | 10/11/06 | | |
| Make sure I can use the software features I will need | Ongoing until start of controlled conditions | 10/01/07 | | |
| Plan what I need and set up folders to save all my work in for this unit | 3/11/06 | 3/11/06 | | |
| Investigate the audience for the newsletter – their interests and knowledge of ICT and the style of presentation they like | Weekend of 10/11 November | 12/11/06 | Can ask questions over the weekend but difficult during the week | |
| Summarise my findings from the investigation and produce evaluation criteria to use to test my newsletter against | 12/13 November | 13 November | | |
| Produce draft designs for layout of the newsletter | 14/11/06 | 16/11/06 | So I have ready for the weekend | |
| Test my draft designs against the relevant evaluation criteria with the audience | 17/18 November | End of the weekend | I can't test my final newsletter with my audience so I have to make sure my designs are suitable | |
| Summarise comments and incorporate into final design | 19/11/06 | 21/11/06 | | |
| Produce a final design for the newsletter | 21/11/06 | 28/11/06 | Think this might take longer than I think | |
| Research content for the newsletter | From 1/11/06 | 10/1/07 | Want all files ready for start of controlled conditions. Will try to look out for articles etc. all the while | |
| Write up content for articles and save as unformatted text files | From 1/11/06 | 10/1/07 | | |
| Get illustrations needed, format and save | From 1/11/06 | 10/1/07 | | |
| Add cross-referencing to files of pictures and text in the final design | 08/01/07 | 08/01/07 | | |
| Complete my bibliography of all research sources used and check against guidance notes on layout of bibliographies | 01/11/06 | 08/01/07 | | |
| Produce screenshot to show all files needed | 09/01/07 | 09/01/07 | Ready for the start of controlled conditions | |
| Make sure this plan is completed for the investigation time before I forget anything | | | | |

**Figure 1.18** An example of part of a student's plan

This table shows the marks allocated in the mark scheme from June 2006 for the time planning.

| 1 mark | 2 marks | 3 marks |
|---|---|---|
| Basic time planning shown. | Time actually spent is recorded. | Time plan clearly shows monitoring of, and amendments to, original version, showing reasons for amendments. |

As you will see, there are only three marks available for the completed time plan. This may not seem to represent many marks, but the plan is important, not only because of the marks allocated to it, but also because, unless you do plan your time carefully and work out what you have got to do, you will lose marks in other areas that you end up rushing or forget to do.

## Investigating the needs of the audience

One of the problems with many ICT solutions that are produced is that the people who produce them think they know what the users want. This is often not the case and the outcome is software that people cannot use, or information produced in a format or style that the audience doesn't like or can't understand. As a result, they don't bother to read it or only skim it and end up with the wrong information. This is why it is so important to spend some time getting to understand the audience for your newsletter (or web pages). If you do you will find the design work much easier and you will be able to produce something that meets the assessment criteria. If you don't understand the audience or what the purpose of the newsletter or web pages is then you will find it very difficult to gain good marks.

When you know what the purpose and audience are for your newsletter or web pages and once you have worked out your time plan, you need to establish what information you will need to put into it and what style of presentation will be most suitable for the audience.

To do this it will be necessary to do some research. First of all look at other web pages or newsletters aimed at the target audience. What can you learn from them? Are there any things in common that obviously work with that audience? Can you get a member of the target audience to look at some examples and tell you what they think of them? (**Items 12a** and **12b** on the CD-ROM show four examples of publications intended for different audiences.)

When you have an idea of the sort of style that is needed for the given audience, make sure that you have the skills in the software to create the features that you will need – you do not want to be trying to find out how to do something for the first time during the controlled conditions because it will always take you longer than you think.

### TASK 18

What are the differences between the four types of publication shown in **Items 12a** and **12b** on the CD-ROM?

## TASK 19

For a newsletter or web pages produced for a local community group, such as a cricket club, playgroup or for a parish magazine, do the following:

1   Find an example of a newsletter produced for that group or some examples of ones produced for other similar groups.
2   Ask some members of the group various questions:
   a   What do they like or dislike about the format the information is produced in?
   b   What do they like or dislike about the fonts and colours used?
   c   If illustrations are used, are they relevant or amusing? Do they add anything?
   d   Is there anything in particular in the information they do or don't like?
   e   Is the content interesting or informative?

Next, try to discover what interests the audience that the newsletter/web pages are intended for, has. What content would interest them? Again, look at other information produced for that particular group. Ideally, you should interview several different people from the audience. For example, in the assignment given above, you would need to find out who belongs to the community group. How old are they? Do they have anything in common? Do they have the same interests? What is their knowledge of ICT like? Have they heard of and do they understand any of the ICT legislation? What sort of things do they use ICT for at present and what might they want to use it for? (See **Item 22** on the CD-ROM for more help on asking questions of your target audience.)

At the end of your work you need to show:

■ evidence of an understanding of the needs of the audience for which the newsletter/web pages are intended, from which the assessment criteria for evaluation are derived.

If you use questionnaires then make sure that you do a summary of what they contain and do not include every copy of the questionnaire, one will do. Also, make sure that they are not all just filled in by you or your friends – this is usually pretty obvious to an examiner!

Remember to say not just **what** is required, but **why**. For example, 'Including information about copyright law would be useful for the members because they have to write articles for publication and a lot of them do not understand what pictures they can use from the Internet and what is illegal to use.'

The table opposite shows the marks available in June 2006 for this section of the work.

## reminder

Don't forget to have a look at the principal examiner's report from previous examinations, which gives information about what the examiners have found that students have done wrong or have failed to do in their work. See:
http://www.aqa.org.uk/qual/gceapplied/ict_exam.html
and **Item 15** on the CD-ROM, which gives the principal examiner's report from June 2006.

| 1 mark | 2 marks | 3 marks |
|---|---|---|
| Candidate has stated who the audience is and explained some of their characteristics. | Candidate has demonstrated a clear understanding of the impact of the needs of the audience on content **or** layout. | Candidate has demonstrated a full understanding of the impact of the needs of the audience on content **and** layout. |

You will notice that to be able to gain the highest marks here you must consider both content **and** layout. You have got to demonstrate in your work that you really do understand the audience for whom you are designing the newsletter/web pages. This is an aspect that on its own does not gain you a lot of marks, but without it you will find that you lose marks elsewhere. This is because you will not be able to justify your designs and your use of features without a clear understanding of the audience and purpose.

## Evaluation criteria

You can only produce your evaluation criteria after you have done the research on the audience and the styles of presentation of information needed. These criteria are statements about what your solution (newsletter or web pages) should be like, what it should contain and how the information should be presented. They are what you should test your designs against and what you will use to assess the success or otherwise of your solution.

They should **not** be a list of requirements or a list of the things that you have got to make or do. This table shows you examples of poor and good criteria, that is, what are **not** acceptable and what **are** acceptable as typical criteria.

| Poor evaluation criteria | Good evaluation criteria | Qualitative or quantitative |
|---|---|---|
| The newsletter should contain text and pictures. | The newsletter should only contain images that are relevant to the articles in it. | Qualitative |
| The newsletter should be easy to read. | The text should be written using terminology that can be understood by … | Qualitative |
| The web pages should contain interesting information. | Information in the newsletter should be based on information that is no older than 3 months. | Quantitative |
| Bullet points should be used in the newsletter. | Images should be at least 4 cm square to aid viewing and clarity. | Quantitative |

Notice that evaluation criteria can be either qualitative or quantitative. Qualitative criteria are based on opinions and quantitative criteria can be measured. So, for a newsletter the only people who can assess it objectively against the qualitative criteria are members of the audience that the newsletter is intended for. This means that testing against these criteria must be carried out during the design phase and before controlled conditions start.

This table shows the marks available for the evaluation criteria from June 2006:

| 1 mark | 2 marks | 3 marks |
|---|---|---|
| Basic evaluation criteria produced for the newsletter. | Appropriate evaluation criteria demonstrating how they are assessing the suitability for purpose and audience. | Clear and appropriate evaluation criteria given. The candidate has described how evaluation criteria were arrived at. |

Note that again how good these criteria are will affect your ability to gain marks on testing and evaluation. Notice also that you are expected to show how you arrived at the evaluation criteria that you are using, in other words:

■ Where did you get them from?
■ What are they based on?

This is where you must refer back to your investigation of the audience.

### Design work

When solving any problem it is important to try to think of several solutions and then work out which is the best one and the most suitable for the situation. In this unit, you will need to come up with up to three different draft designs for a newsletter or web pages. The draft designs may have slightly different styles to them, they could have different information in them or they could have information positioned in different places on the pages, or on different pages.

**reminder**

Design work should either be done by hand – often quicker and easier, particularly for draft designs – or it should be produced in different software to the software that you will use to produce your final template and newsletter/web pages during controlled conditions. If you use software to produce the designs you **must** state what program you have used. It is not sufficient to simply print out several alternative templates that are available with the final software used. Make sure that all design work is clearly labelled as 'draft' or 'final' and is separate to the implementation of the final newsletter.

### TASK 20

Use the example exercise in **Item 16** on the CD-ROM to practise drawing draft designs and producing suitable evaluation criteria to assess their suitability. Figures 1.25 and 1.26 show what draft designs should look like. (These are also provided as **Items 17a** and **17b** on the CD-ROM.)

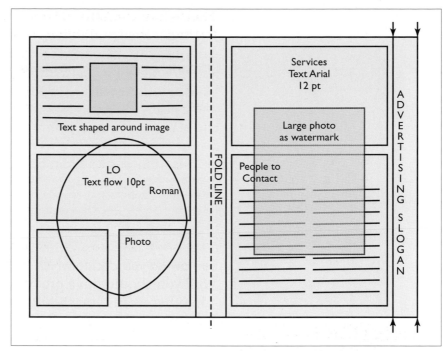

**Figure 1.19** Example of a draft design

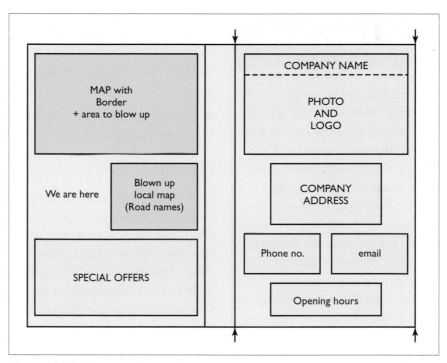

**Figure 1.20** Example of a draft design

This table shows the marks available for the draft designs and testing of their suitability in the June 2006 mark scheme:

| 1 mark | 2 marks | 3 marks |
|---|---|---|
| Candidate has produced draft designs. | Candidate has produced annotated draft designs. | Candidate has clearly shown understanding of the target audience in their annotated draft designs. |
| Some evidence of testing draft designs. | Good evidence and understanding of how draft designs were tested. | |

### So how do you decide which draft design is the best one?

Well you should have produced some evaluation criteria now – in other words you should know what will best suit the audience and purpose of the newsletter/web pages. This means that you can compare each of your draft designs against your criteria and see which is 'the best fit', i.e. satisfies most if not all of the criteria.

As you are still working during the investigation time, you can take the opportunity to show the designs to some of the target audience and get their reactions. This is what is defined as 'testing'. The following is the requirement for that to be done in the work that is handed in:

■ Evidence of testing the draft designs of the newsletter/web pages and any steps taken to correct errors and/or make other changes to try to ensure that the needs of the audience have been met.

It is important that the evidence you put in to your work is clear – it shows exactly what you have done and why. All too often students lose marks here because they have not shown their evidence clearly. They stick in some very badly drawn draft designs that have been rushed off at the last minute, just to include something. It is also important that if you have shown items to members of the target audience you have clear evidence to show this, so what you have done separates you off from the student who has just got their friend to fill in a few questionnaires!

### So what is a final design?

A final design is one that could be given to someone else with knowledge of the software and that contains sufficient detail for that person to be able to create the solution **exactly**.

Exactly means that every dimension will be exactly as in the design. The colours, font sizes, styles, bullets, watermarking, positioning of labels, content of articles, etc. will be the same. It must not be approximately the same size or about the same colour but exactly so. Precision is very important in ICT and

## reminder

You are never asked to produce something just to make you jump through hoops. There is always a reason for doing things and in most cases it is because this is exactly what you would do in real life. People want to see alternatives and you do not want to waste time by producing each of these in detail, so you do several draft designs and then when the decision is made you produce one final design in detail.

when people can't be bothered to be precise, solutions are created that don't provide exactly what is needed! The requirement for this detailed design work is one of the things that you will find different studying a course at this level from GCSE.

## TASK 21

**Item 18** on the CD-ROM is a page from a book. What information would you need to find out to be able to produce an **exact** replica of the page?

Produce a final design for this page that you could give to someone who hasn't seen it so that they could reproduce it exactly.

It is very important that you show on a copy of your final design why you are presenting the information in the way that you are. If you do not do this then even if your design could be implemented by someone else (a third party) you will still not be able to gain all of the marks.

This means that you must annotate your design and/or include some writing with it which explains your choice of features used in the final design. For example, if you have used a two-column format for a newsletter, why has this style been chosen? Does it make it easier to read? Why have you broken up text with images? Does this help to keep someone's concentration? Some people might find this irritating and only want pictures at the start or end of an article. Which of those is most effective and why? You need to explain how the way that you are going to display the information is appropriate for the audience and task as this gains you marks for A03 Application of knowledge and understanding.

This final design is for the template(s) that you are going to produce for the newsletter or web pages, with the actual content being shown as references to data files, containing text or pictures. Figure 1.21 shows an example of a final design. This is also included as **Item 19** on the CD-ROM.

The table on page 44 shows the rows from the June 2006 mark scheme which were assessing the final design. You can see that there were eight marks allocated to the design. The first four marks are for how detailed the design itself is (and therefore how easy it is for a third person to implement) and the range of features used. The second four marks are available for how well you have annotated the design and demonstrated your understanding of designing for a particular purpose and audience.

## important note

If you are producing a set of web pages or a newsletter with several identically formatted pages that will have different content then you will only need to draw a detailed final design for one page and then explain how the content will vary from page to page. Also remember that a design should include a diagram to show how the pages link together.

The full mark scheme is also shown on the CD-ROM – **Item 14**. A good, detailed, well-annotated design will help you in the controlled conditions as well as gaining you marks.

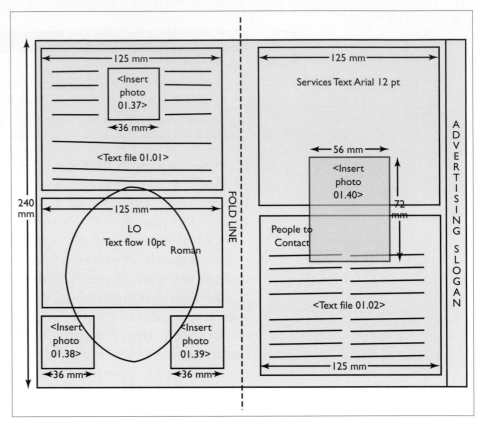

**Figure 1.21** An example of a final design

| 1 mark | 2 marks | 3 marks | 4 marks |
|---|---|---|---|
| Final design has been produced but could not be implemented by a third party. | Final design shows a range of features but could not be implemented by a third party. | Final design produced that could be implemented by a third party but uses few design features. | Detailed final design that could easily be implemented by a third party and clearly shows a range of features. |
| Candidate has annotated the final design. | In the annotation of the final design the candidate explains why some features have been used. | The annotation of the final design explains why all of the features have been used. | The fully annotated final design clearly demonstrates a range of features and suitability for the audience and purpose. |

## Researching the content

The candidate instructions that you receive will include something like:

Your work must contain:

▶ a final design for the format and structure of the newsletter/web pages to show evidence of your planning.

It should be clear where all of the information that is going to be included in the newsletter or web pages is coming from and where it can be found. This means that you need to provide:

▶ a listing of files containing pre-prepared research material to be used during controlled conditions.

What the examination board want you to do is to carry out all of your research and find all of the content to put into the newsletter or web pages before you begin your controlled conditions sessions. This means that you will not be wasting any time during the controlled conditions sessions and also ensures that you're not able to just copy material straight off the Internet or from books or magazines. The reason for this is that they want to see that you understand what the effects of ICT on society are. You cannot do this if you simply copy something word for word from a book. You need to write things in your own words in order to make the information in the newsletter or web pages relevant to the particular audience for which it is intended. It also means there is a need to put the information into a suitable format.

So, once you know what the task is and who the information is for, and you have done your research into the audience and their needs, then you can start to look for relevant information and write the content you will need to put into your template when you create it from your design during the controlled conditions.

You must remember that information can be found in lots of different places and you should not just rely on what you find on the Internet. You will not get the highest marks if this is all that you do! The instructions that you receive at the start of the investigation time will give you possible types of sources that you could use for research. (See **Item 13** on the CD-ROM.)

The evidence that you have conducted research will come from the content that you incorporate into the newsletter and also from the bibliography that you put together for inclusion. On the following page are the marks awarded for the bibliography in the June 2006 examination.

**Figure 1.22** Remember to use a range of sources

| 1 mark | 2 marks |
|---|---|
| Candidate has shown some evidence of a bibliography. | Candidate has used at least two different types of research sources. |
| Candidate has produced a bibliography that contains the detail as recommended in the Candidate Booklet. | |

'Types of research sources' means the Internet, books, magazines, interviews, television programmes, and so on. The Candidate Booklet will contain the guidelines on what detail should be included for what type of source. (See also **Item 5** and **Item 6** on the CD-ROM.) If you don't do these things then you are throwing away very straightforward marks.

Look at past tasks and see what the information that you include in the newsletter or web pages has to show. It will probably be something like:

For each example that you use the content must:

▶ show a suitable example relevant to the audience
▶ be factually correct
▶ ensure that advantages and/or disadvantages to the audience are given
▶ show the source of the information clearly.

Remember to make sure that you know exactly how many examples you need to include on what. The numbers may change from one task in one examination sitting to another. You may need to include one example of how legislation concerned with using ICT affects the target audience, or it may be two examples. You might be asked to consider people with particular needs for one task but not for another. Check and re-check what the task given to you in the Candidate Booklet says. Look at how many marks are allocated to the content of the newsletter – to the examples, and make sure you are absolutely clear on what each example must show. When you have written your content, check that it does explain exactly what is asked for, that any advantages or disadvantages are clear, that it is factually correct and that you have indicated your source if you need to.

Below is an example of an article from a newsletter that was written for the home computer user which had to include information on developments in ICT.

---

Wireless networks are becoming much more commonly used in private houses.[1] Many families will now have more than one computer in the house and will need, or want to, share data and access to external networks using a wireless network. Using a wireless network rather than one that requires wires to connect the network stations together has the advantages that network stations can be located anywhere within range. There are no unsightly wires required and the cost of installation is also reduced.

There are, however, disadvantages, and the main disadvantage is security issues. Very few households are aware of the fact that gaining access to a wireless network is much easier than one based on wires. All that a hacker needs to do is to intercept the signals.

"I didn't realise I needed to have my own Internet access," said one student I interviewed.

"I was gaining access through the wireless network they had in the flat upstairs!"

Mr Jason from PJC computer systems said, "Many people just have no idea of the risks they are taking when they install a wireless network in their homes."

[1] See *CompuTimes* 3 May 2006

In the article taken from a newsletter shown above you can see that all of the exam requirements are met. The content is relevant, factually correct, and shows the advantages and disadvantages. Also, the source of facts is clearly stated using a footnote – here the student has given the name and date of the actual newspaper article used.

**Figure 1.23** Remember you can gain information from interviews

Do remember that the source of all information used does not have to be a piece of written material. You may have interviewed someone and want to include a quotation from them.

You could have found some information in a television program or in a video that you have watched. Just make sure that you properly give the source of whatever you include.

### How to be organised

Each of the separate articles or diagrams, pictures, or graphs that you want to use should be saved in a different file in a folder that you create specifically for your work relating to the assignment. You should give the files sensible names so that they could be easily understood by someone else building up the newsletter or web pages from your design.

All files containing text **must** be saved as plain text files without any formatting in them. This means that they should have the extension .txt. They can be created using software such as Microsoft® Notepad™, or they can be saved in plain text format in a word processing program.

You do **not** need to print out the content of these files. The content will be marked from the copy of the final newsletter that you produce during the controlled conditions.

The important thing to remember is that plain text is text without formatting. The formatting that is required for each file should be set up in the template that you produce. This is to ensure that as you insert the text from your text file into the relevant text box in your template it will automatically be formatted as you designed it to be.

## definition

**Rich Text**

Rich Text – a standard formalised by Microsoft Corporation for specifying formatting of documents. RTF files are actually ASCII files with special commands to indicate formatting information, such as fonts and margins. Other document formatting languages include the Hypertext Markup Language (HTML), which is used to define documents on the World Wide Web, and the Standard Generalised Markup Language (SGML), which is a more robust version of HTML.

**Plain text**

Plain text – refers to textual data in ASCII format. Plain text is the most portable format because it is supported by nearly every application on every machine. It is quite limited, however, because it cannot contain any formatting commands.

*Source*: Wikipedia

You will need to take two copies of the screenshots of the file lists that you used so that you can use one to show the files as they appeared when you started the controlled conditions (row 1 in the table below) and a second that is annotated. This is to show the examiner which files you used and any extra files that you decided that you needed part-way through the controlled conditions (row 2 below). See **Item 20a** and **Item 20b** on the CD-ROM for examples of screenshots of lists of files.

The following table shows the marks allocated to these items of proof from the June 2006 mark scheme:

| 1 mark | 2 marks |
|---|---|
| Candidate has produced a screenshot(s) of all of the files of researched material to be used under controlled conditions. | |
| Candidate has included a screenshot(s) of the files of researched material that they **used** during controlled conditions. | Candidate has included a screenshot(s) of the files of researched material that they **used** during controlled conditions, annotated to show amendments and additions to the initial list. |

### Standard ways of working

Standard ways of working in this unit examines the way in which you store and name files and whether you understand conventions for file naming and have adopted a suitable one for each file. It is particularly important with this unit because you have to submit all of the files of content to your teacher in electronic format before you start the controlled conditions. If you find that you need extra information later on you can add

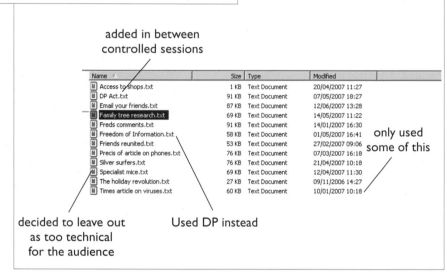

| Name | Size | Type |
|---|---|---|
| mouse.pcx | 202KB | PC Paintbrush Image |
| mobile.fpx | 96KB | Microsoft Picture It! Picture |
| bakground page1.jpg | 349KB | JPEG Image |
| holiday background.jpg | 12KB | JPEG Image |
| Fred.tif | 292KB | TIF Image Document |
| friends.gif | 4KB | GIF Image |
| virus cartoon.bmp | 62KB | Bitmap Image |
| shopping arcade.JPG | 17KB | JPEG Image |
| live mouse.mix | 168KB | Microsoft PhotoDraw Picture |
| title banner.bmp | 282KB | Bitmap Image |
| BJT.png | 30KB | PNG Image |
| my cartoon.jpg | 52KB | JPEG Image |

I used all of the files, as can be seen in my designs and how the newsletter was built up.

added in between controlled sessions

| Name | Size | Type | Modified | |
|---|---|---|---|---|
| Access to shops.txt | 1 KB | Text Document | 20/04/2007 11:27 | |
| DP Act.txt | 91 KB | Text Document | 07/05/2007 18:27 | |
| Email your friends.txt | 87 KB | Text Document | 12/06/2007 13:28 | |
| Family tree research.txt | 69 KB | Text Document | 14/05/2007 11:22 | |
| Freds comments.txt | 91 KB | Text Document | 14/01/2007 16:30 | |
| Freedom of Information.txt | 58 KB | Text Document | 01/05/2007 16:41 | only used |
| Friends reunited.txt | 53 KB | Text Document | 27/02/2007 09:06 | some of this |
| Precis of article on phones.txt | 76 KB | Text Document | 07/03/2007 16:18 | |
| Silver surfers.txt | 76 KB | Text Document | 21/04/2007 10:18 | |
| Specialist mice.txt | 69 KB | Text Document | 12/04/2007 11:30 | |
| The holiday revolution.txt | 27 KB | Text Document | 09/11/2006 14:27 | |
| Times article on viruses.txt | 60 KB | Text Document | 10/01/2007 10:18 | |

decided to leave out as too technical for the audience

Used DP instead

**Figure 1.24** Examples of screenshots of the file lists

to your list of files. Again, you should do this by giving the file to the teacher to check first. You may also prepare more content than you actually need. This does not matter because you can simply indicate on the printout which files you didn't use, or add on by hand the extra ones that you had to produce. This will be marked from the lists of files detailed above.

## Bibliography

Finally, before you go into the controlled conditions you must make sure that you have produced a bibliography. The candidate instructions that you receive will say something like:

> ► A detailed bibliography listing the sources used while researching and gathering the material to be used for the newsletter/web pages.

You must create this bibliography in the way that is specified by the examination board in the candidate instructions. See the earlier notes on this on page 11 and pages 45–6 and also **Item 5** and **Item 6** on the CD-ROM.

As you go along, you should add to the bibliography every reference source that you use, as you use it. So start by creating a file for your bibliography that you can add things to easily. Think about formatting this as a table so you make sure you include everything that is required.

### Ready for the controlled conditions

This is what you should now have in a folder ready for the controlled conditions.

### As paper copies:

1. Your candidate booklet.
2. A plan for the work to be done.
3. A record to show whether this plan has been followed and any adjustments made in order to complete the tasks – filled in up to the start of the controlled conditions.
4. Evidence of an understanding of the needs of the audience for which the newsletter/web pages are being produced.
5. The evaluation criteria for the newsletter/web pages.
6. The draft designs.
7. Evidence of testing the draft designs of the newsletter/web pages.
8. A final design for the format and structure of the newsletter/web pages, annotated to show use of features and suitability for audience and purpose, and including references to the files of content.
9. A detailed bibliography.
10. Two copies of the listings of files containing pre-prepared research material.

### In electronic format:

1. All of the files of text and pictures that you think you will need to complete the newsletter

This list is included as **Item 21** on the CD-ROM.

## Controlled conditions

### The template

The first thing that you must do when you get into the controlled conditions is to work through your final design and create a template(s) into which you will place the information from your research files. This is where having spent time learning the software before the controlled conditions will pay off – you will find it much quicker to create the template(s) if you know exactly how to do things! It will also help you if you have a good detailed design prepared, which you can simply follow, because trying to think how you want to present the information when you are already in controlled conditions would not be easy.

Think of the template as a series of spaces that will need filling. Each space must be formatted in the way that you have specified in your design, so this will mean setting, for example, colours, font types and sizes, borders, outlines, bullets and possibly watermarks which will then be applied to any information that you add into the space. A sample template has been set up on the CD-ROM for you to view – **Item 23**.

When you have completed your template(s) you must print them off and annotate them to show what you have set up in each space and to prove that you have used the functions (or features) available in the software. This will count towards your marks for A01 Practical capability in applying ICT.

The following table shows the marks available for the template in the June 2006 examination:

| I mark | 2 marks | 3 marks |
|---|---|---|
| Candidate has produced a screenshot/printouts of template(s). | Candidate has produced annotated screenshots/printouts of templates and has pointed out a number of features. | Candidate has produced fully annotated screenshots/printouts, including fonts, margins, page sizes, styles, etc. Candidate has explained most of the features used in the context of the newsletter. |
| Candidate has shown some evidence of using software features. | Candidate has demonstrated use of a number of software features, and related these to audience and purpose. | Candidate has shown a very clear understanding of why the features are fit for purpose and audience. |

It is important that you understand that the marks here are for using the software to create the templates. The marks in the final design are for designing what effects you want; this is about actually achieving them. That is why the evidence that you use for the final design must be completely separate from the evidence that you provide to show the implementation of your templates. Do make sure that all printouts are easily legible and are clearly labelled as template printouts.

## Adding the information to the template

When you have completed the template the next stage is to add in the pictures and text from your research files. You need to show a series of:

■ screenshots to show how the newsletter/web pages was/were composed and developed, cross-referenced to the research files.

This means that an examiner can tell which file on your list of files has been used in which space of your template. You may also be using layering, where text is overlaid onto a picture or you may find that you need to resize images to fit into the spaces you have created in your template for them. All of these actions need to be illustrated using screenshots. You will probably find the easiest way to do this is by having a word processing file open into which you save your screenshots as you go along, adding in text to explain what each screenshot shows. Do be careful that you only include the minimum number of screenshots; the examiner does not need to know how to use the software. So it is about the composition of material in the template, not how you selected menu $x$ and option $y$ from the software functions.

**Figure 1.25** Resizing a vector graphic

**Figure 1.26** Resizing a bitmapped graphic

The following table shows the marks allocated for this part of the work, composing the newsletter/web pages, in the June 2006 examination:

| 1 mark | 2 marks | 3 marks |
|---|---|---|
| Candidate has produced a series of screenshots displaying their work. | Candidate has produced a series of annotated screenshots showing how their work was built up. | Candidate has produced a set of fully annotated screenshots demonstrating clearly stages of composition and development by, for example, enhancing or rejecting images. |
| Candidate has produced some evidence of cross-referencing newsletter content to research. | Candidate has demonstrated how their research files have been used in their finished work. | Candidate has fully matched what they have produced to their research work. It is possible to see where all of the content has come from. |

The first row of this table shows the marks available for demonstrating that you have produced the templates. The second row shows the marks that relate to your being able to show how each file that you use has been used and where it has been placed in the template. The research files referred to are the files of content, text and pictures that you prepared during the investigation time. This is **not** about showing the source of the information in those files.

## Making changes to your design

You must keep a careful note of any changes that you have had to make to your final design and why these changes were necessary. It may be something like the colour that you have chosen for a background is too dark to show up the writing superimposed on it. It could be that the picture you had selected isn't clear enough when it is resized to fit into a particular space. You may need to shorten some of the text because there isn't enough space to fit it all in. All of these things will need to be mentioned in your evaluation. Again the message is be honest, don't pretend you got everything to work perfectly – very few people do. Obviously the better your knowledge of the software when you created your final design, the less chance there is that you will have to make many alterations to the design. The more you think about the content in advance the less likelihood there is that you will need to alter it at this point.

## When you have finished

When you have a completed newsletter or set of web pages you must print it out as you would want it to look. You will need to provide:

■ a printout of the completed newsletter/web pages.

Always remember that if the newsletter is going to be A5 size, but you are creating A4 pages, you will need to fold the finished pages and put them together correctly – make sure you have left good-sized margins for doing this!

The completed newsletter or web pages are what an examiner will use to mark the content. The marks for the content will be worth about a third of the total marks for the portfolio. This is because this unit is about ICT and society and it is the content of the newsletter that shows whether you understand what effects ICT is having on a particular section of society – the audience for the newsletter or web pages.

## Evaluation of the newsletter/web pages

As mentioned in the introduction to this book, one of the key skills that anyone must have is the ability to evaluate objectively what they have produced. It does not matter whether this is an ICT solution or the performance a player puts in during a football game. Whatever the context is, the ability to reflect upon and judge the quality of what has been achieved is a skill. It is an important skill that is required by employers because they want people to be able to evaluate what they have produced so that they can improve it next time.

You will have set some evaluation criteria for your newsletter or web pages against which you should now measure the success of the newsletter or web pages in achieving the aims you set out. To do this logically you should do the following:

■ Look at each evaluation criterion in turn.
■ Ask yourself:
  – Has this been met or not?
  – Where is the evidence to show whether or not it has been met?
  – If it hasn't been met, why not?

If you write up your evaluation of the newsletter or web pages in this way, taking each criterion in turn and quoting evidence or reasons for success or failure, then you will produce a good quality evaluation.

This is an easy part of the work to gain marks on. What examiners do not want to see is the student who just states 'I think' or 'as you can see it meets the evaluation criteria' without showing any real understanding or providing evidence to back up what they are saying. You are required to produce:

■ an evaluation of the newsletter/web pages produced, using evidence from testing to show that the audience needs and the evaluation criteria have, or have not, been met.

This table shows the marks allocated to evaluation of the newsletter in the June 2006 examination:

| I mark | 2 marks | 3 marks |
|---|---|---|
| Basic evaluation produced of how the newsletter is suitable for the audience. | Clear evaluation produced of how the newsletter is suitable for the audience and purpose. | Comprehensive evaluation produced clearly demonstrating how the newsletter is suitable for the audience and purpose. Reference is made to the original criteria. |

Make sure that you avoid the 'I think' type of comment by making reference to the evidence that you have in your portfolio. For example, if you did some testing with your target audience, refer to it. If you had a summary of a questionnaire that you used, then mention it. Also, refer to the screenshots that show your template or the composition of the newsletter.

## Evaluating your own performance

You must produce:

■ an evaluation of your own performance in completing the work and following your plan.

For this again you need to be honest. As mentioned previously it is not always easy to be critical of yourself and what you have done, and being able to admit that you have made mistakes is difficult.

This table shows the marks given in the June 2006 examination for the candidate's evaluation of their own performance:

| I mark | 2 marks | 3 marks |
|---|---|---|
| Basic evaluation of candidate performance. | Evaluation produced showing how problems were overcome. Appropriate reference made to screenshots of development. | Clear and complete evaluation giving detailed explanations and clear evidence of problems overcome, all referenced to screenshots of development or time plan. |

In order to gain a good mark for this evaluation you need to look at everything you have done from the start of the controlled conditions time and decide where you could have made improvements:

- Was there anything you didn't spend enough time on?
- Were your designs as good as they should have been or did you have difficulty following them in the controlled conditions?
- Did you find enough content for your newsletter or did you waste your time and end up having to find more between the controlled conditions sessions?
- Did you spend enough time and do enough research to have a clear idea of what would be suitable for the audience?
- Did you actually speak to anyone from the target audience or did you think you knew about their needs without having to bother to do this?

In particular, use your time plan to help highlight any of the places where you were weaker or had to amend the plan. Also, remember to listen to the comments that your teacher makes about your work or the way in which you approached it.

Higher marks are gained by students who are honest, not those who try to pretend everything they did was perfect! Make sure that, as for the evaluation of the work, you provide evidence by saying 'as can be seen in the time plan', or 'the screenshots of the development of the template show that I had problems …'.

### Final things to do

When you have finished writing your evaluations, get both copies of the printout showing the lists of files that you took into the controlled conditions and submitted to your teacher, and annotate one copy of them so that you have:

- a list of all the files used, annotated to show amendments and additions to the initial list (see the annotated file lists on page 50 as an example of this).

If there are any files you didn't use, say why not, and don't forget to add on any extra files that you needed. Remember, you must give reasons for the changes you have had to make.

If you used exactly what you submitted then it is very important that you actually say this otherwise the examiner will think that you didn't have time to do any annotation or have ignored this part of the instructions!

## reminder

Don't forget to leave enough time to do the evaluation – about a tenth of the marks are available for this – just the sort of thing that can make the difference of one or even two grades!

## Getting the work together for handing in

Now put everything together. Make sure that:

- all work has your name and candidate number on it
- all items are labelled as in the candidate booklet
- you have checked that you have done everything
- if you have time, go back and check that everything that should be annotated is annotated
- all of your printouts are clear
- the work is in order.

Don't waste any spare time that you have, make sure you improve anything that you can in the time available.
    And …

## Afterwards

Try to remember any mistakes that you may have made in your time planning in particular, or in the quality of your design work, evaluation criteria or testing. These are all things which you will have to do again in other units that you study, so learn from your mistakes! That is what you are supposed to be doing and what employers want employees to be able to do. Nobody expects perfection, particularly the first time, but you should still aim for it!

# 2 ICT and organisations

**The specification for this unit states that this unit will help you to:**

▶ understand the information needs of organisations

▶ understand how organisations, both large and small, public and commercial, are structured

▶ understand how developments in technology affect how organisations collect information and how that information flows within and between organisations

▶ understand how developments in technology affect why and how organisations present information

▶ consider how ICT systems support different activities or functions within organisations

▶ evaluate the effectiveness of ICT systems in helping organisations achieve their goals

This unit is a really important one because you need to understand why and how ICT is used in organisations today. Often in organisations the employees who are most valuable to the organisation are not those who are the technical ICT experts, but those who understand how ICT can be used to benefit the organisation. Technical experts can always be brought in, but someone who can recognise the opportunity for increasing revenue by introducing a new ICT system is something that is much more difficult to find. Examples of what is meant by this are given in the following two case studies.

## case study 1

**Figure 2.1** Veterinary clinic

Company X sells pharmaceutical drugs to veterinary surgeries worldwide. They have become one of the largest companies in this field by using ICT. One of their sales representatives who visited the vets at their surgeries noticed that every time the vet wanted to put in an order he had to include all of the details of every drug that they needed. There are many drugs that are used on a daily basis for things like routine injections, and having to complete an order every time was a waste of the vet's time. He suggested to the company that they emailed the vets a 'normal' order so that all the vet had to do was to confirm it or make amendments to it or add extra items on and email it back to the company. This made the vets much more inclined to order from this supplier because the time saved was quite great when added up over a year. The result was an increase in the company's profits. The sales representative ended up as a senior manager travelling around the world!

**case study 2**

A company that is a major distributor of goods around the world was concerned that they were not keeping staff for any great length of time. The personnel section found out that there was little staff loyalty because the staff did not really know much about the company. One of the personnel staff suggested that the company could produce a newsletter 'in-house' using a desktop publishing package. This newsletter would help to keep all of the staff aware of what was happening and tell them about significant events like people getting married, or the company winning awards or orders. The company started with this idea and then developed it into a staff section on the company intranet. The result – staff who now feel part of the company and considerably reduced turnover of staff, resulting in lower costs and higher productivity for the company.

# Assessment for this unit

▶ You will have to produce a portfolio of work to provide evidence for assessment. You will be assessed against the four assessment objectives:

■ A01 Practical capability in applying ICT (21 marks)
■ A02 Knowledge and understanding of ICT systems and their roles in organisations and society (21 marks)
■ A03 Application of knowledge, skills and understanding to produce solutions to ICT problems (14 marks)
■ A04 Evaluation of ICT solutions and your own performance (14 marks)

These objectives are the same for all of the units that you will study. What changes is the weighting on the different objectives so, for example, A02 has less weighting in Unit 2 than in Unit 1 and A01 has a higher weighting in this unit than in Unit 1.

As this is an internally assessed unit, the assessment of your work is carried out by your teacher. Then the standard of your school's marking is checked by the examination board to make sure that all marking in different schools and colleges across the country is to the same standard. Notice that the number of marks for your practical skills is only 21 out of the possible 70, so you cannot get away with just being good at using a piece of software. Showing what you understand in your writing is very important, as is the way that you plan and carry out your work.

# Background knowledge needed

When starting off on this unit it is really important to remember what ICT is and what is meant by an organisation.

As an organisation is a system, information will go into it, be moved around and processed, used within it and output from it. Different types of organisation may require information for different purposes. They use this information to serve their own particular purpose. This is what is meant by the 'information processing needs' of an organisation, a phrase used in the specification and marking scheme for this unit.

## Thinking about organisations

### The information needs of organisations

Remember what was said earlier in this book – that ICT does not really allow any organisation to do anything new. Organisations have been producing and moving information around for hundreds of years, they have just done it in different ways and, in the past, a lot slower and in smaller quantities than is currently possible. It does not matter whether an organisation is large or small, public or private, it will still need to handle information to fulfil its purpose.

### Does organisation size matter?

In a few words, not a lot. Consider the two following case studies. The two organisations are of different sizes, but both perform the same function.

## case study 3
### ▶ Corner shop

The owners of a small shop will check their stock either daily or weekly by looking at the shelves to see what items they have run out of or are low on. They will then check their storeroom to see if they have got any spare stock of these items and if not they will make a list of the items that they need. They will probably make the list on a piece of paper or possibly on a PDA or may even just memorise it. The owner will take a trip to the local cash-and-carry or their wholesaler and buy the items that they need for the next week, probably paying in cash or by cheque. If they forget something or the shop runs out of an item then a quick trip back to the cash-and-carry will resolve the problem and it is unlikely that many customers will be dissatisfied. This is a very informal way of doing things.

**Figure 2.2** Corner shop

## case study 4
### ▶ Supermarket

**Figure 2.3** Supermarket

A supermarket, because of its size, cannot afford to operate in such an informal way. It is probably supplied by a whole range of wholesalers delivering at different times, from all over the country or abroad, or it has a regular scheduled delivery from a central warehouse. If it runs out of an item it may take quite a long time to get the stock. It's not just a case of popping down to the local cash-and-carry. If it does run out of a stock item then the delay could result in many dissatisfied customers. This in turn will result in a loss of profits because customers are either unable to buy the goods they want or decide to shop elsewhere.

A supermarket usually carries a large range of items, which makes it difficult to check all of the items manually or record by hand what needs ordering. So there will need to be some kind of system in place to carry out the activities needed to check the stock, place orders when re-order levels are reached and then send these off to the right supplier or to the central warehouse. It is likely that all of these activities will be carried out using ICT and that payments will also be made electronically using EDI and the BACS system.

## definition

**EDI**
Electronic Data Interchange

**BACS**
Bankers Automated Clearing System

## reminder

Item **URLs** on the CD-ROM has a list of all the web addresses referenced in this book.

## definition

**Infrastructure**
The basic facilities, services, and installations needed for the functioning of ICT systems.

## TASK 1

For case studies 3 and 4:

1  Make a list of what information is needed.
2  Looking at your lists, is the information mainly the same or quite different for the two case studies?

Sainsbury's supermarket chain suffered from a supply problem and problems with their ICT systems at one time. See:

- http://management.silicon.com/itdirector/0,39024673,39125085,00.htm
  for the problems
- http://www.eqos.com/casestudy_sainsbury.shtml
  for how they have used ICT to improve them.

### The bigger the organisation gets …

As you will now have seen, the size of the organisation does not affect what information is needed so much as the complexity in the way the information is moved around, the volume of information and the distances the information has to travel. As the size of an organisation increases, there will be an increase in the number of people involved in information handling. These things mean that there will be differences in the ICT infrastructure depending on the size and scale of the organisation. However, the basic information and what it is used for will be the same for two organisations with the same purpose, regardless of their size.

Item 24 on the CD-ROM includes some information sources and some exercises for you to complete in order to improve your understanding of different types and sizes of organisations, and the information that they use.

### Different types of organisations

Organisations come in different shapes and sizes, and have different reasons for existing. Commercial organisations are just that – they exist for commercial gain. They aim to make money, either for an individual or group of individuals (generally if they are small organisations) or for shareholders (if they are large organisations). Public organisations exist to provide a service to the public and their aim is to make neither a profit nor a loss, but just to 'break even'. What is important for you to remember is that all organisations, whether public or private, need information to be able to exist.

## TASK 2

1    Find definitions for the following terms:
- sole trader
- partnership
- limited company
- shareholder
- utility company
- public company
- private company
- multinational.

Item 25 on the CD-ROM contains a table for you to use to record your definitions.

2    List as many examples of local public and private organisations (both large and small) that you can think of, indicating what service they provide, what they produce, etc. This will help you to think about local organisations that you could possibly investigate for your portfolio work.

### Functions within an organisation

As an organisation gets bigger and more complex it is often necessary to break the organisation down into smaller parts. These become departments or sections, with each one carrying out one particular function or job for the organisation. Sometimes, rather than breaking down an organisation into departments such as sales, production and marketing, the organisation will be split by location, e.g. Manchester, Birmingham and London offices, or by project, e.g. the Atlas project, the front-line project, the brewery project, etc. Organisations make use of a department or project structure because it makes the organisation easier to manage as it gets bigger and bigger.

## TASK 3

Look up in the specification the different functions that organisations need to perform. There is a list in the specification for this unit. (You can find this at: http://www.aqa.org.uk/qual/gceapplied/ict).

Do you understand what all of these mean? Would you know what was involved in each function? You are not expected to have a detailed understanding of every function, but to have an idea of what they are and what happens in, for instance, a personnel department. Remember this is **not** a business studies unit, but an ICT unit! So all of the time you must be looking at how ICT helps organisations carry out each function.

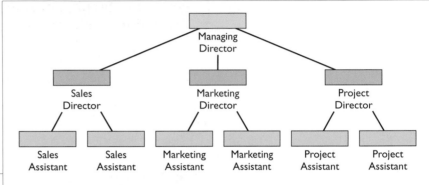

**Figure 2.4** A wide and low organisation structure

The way that an organisation is structured can have an important impact on the way in which information is moved around the organisation. Some organisations have what is known as a wide and low structure and others are tall and narrow. The structure of an organisation is frequently shown in an organisation structure chart. You will find it useful to be able to draw one of these for the organisation that you chose to do your report for, in the assessable part of this unit.

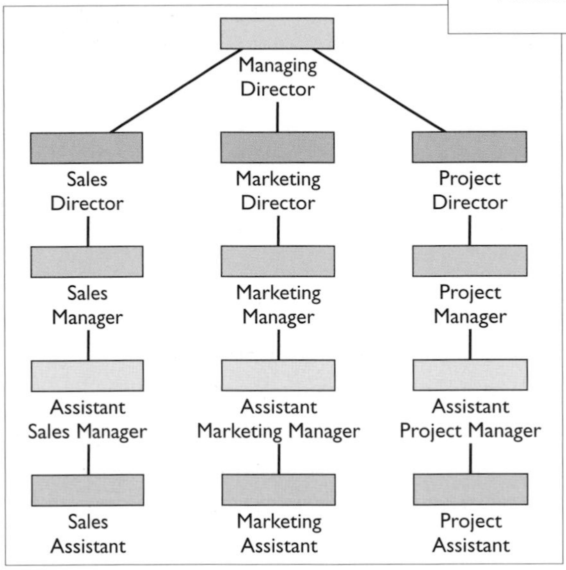


**Figure 2.5** A tall and narrow organisation structure

## reminder

You basically need to understand the following:

- Organisations can have different structures.
- The type of structure can influence the way in which information moves within the organisation.

This is just background information. This is not a business studies unit and it is important that all of the time you are working on this unit you always think, 'So what does this mean in terms of information and ICT?' Students who forget to do this don't get very good marks!

## Levels in organisations

Strategic, tactical and operational are all levels of management/information within an organisation:

- **Strategic** managers are concerned with looking at the 'bigger picture' and long-term goals. An example would be the board of directors/senior managers of a retail company needing information to help them to decide on whether to open stores overseas.
- **Tactical** management is about achieving specific objectives or solving a specific problem. For example, the overseas manager will need information to help them to identify potential sites for new stores.
- **Operational** management is about putting the tactics to work, ensuring things get done. For example, project managers will be responsible for the construction and setting up of the new stores and will need all sorts of information to help them to manage this.

 There is an example of a company structure on the CD-ROM (**Item 26**).

### TASK 1

Draw a structure chart for:

- a local organisation with which you are familiar, e.g. a supermarket or fast food store
- your school or college.

## reminder

When you are doing Task 4 above you are breaking down a large organisation into smaller chunks. **Item 27** on the CD-ROM is an exercise for you to do that will help you see what is meant by the skill of being able to break things down into smaller units, and to see why organisations do this.

## Thinking about information

### What information does an organisation need?

Organisations today rely on having large amounts of information available to them. This is not just the case for the large multinational organisations, but also the small non-profit making ones as well. For example, the local tennis club will need information on:

- names and addresses of members
- phone numbers of members
- skill of members
- location of tennis courts
- direction details for finding them
- points systems for the local league
- details of other team secretaries in the league
- rules of the game
- equipment suppliers
- membership fees
- payments for refreshments and court fees
- general accounting information.

And this list could go on a lot further …!

## TASK 5

Write a list of all of the different information needed by the examinations office in your school or college.

## definition

**Internal information**

Internal information is information that an organisation needs for its internal functions. This information is generated by the organisation itself and moves around within the organisation.

**External information**

External information is information that the organisation needs to get from other outside organisations or individuals, and information that it needs to produce to give to people outside of the organisation or to other organisations.

The following case studies give examples of what internal and external information means for two different types of organisation, one of which is a commercial organisation and one that is not.

## case study 5
### ▶ A commercial organisation

Topjobs is a small landscape gardening company. It's owned by Mr and Mrs Hitchmough and employs three staff. They work for individual clients doing garden maintenance and construction work.

Examples of internal information that the company will generate include:

- jobs to be done
- hours worked by each member of staff
- materials used
- time plans and garden plans for work
- equipment owned and service requirements.

Examples of external information include:

- VAT rate, National Insurance, tax details
- suppliers' information, materials supplied, costs and quantities
- health and safety regulations
- employment regulations
- invoices for customers
- customer information
- hire costs for equipment not owned
- prices charged by competitors
- advertising costs.

## case study 6
### ▶ A charity

The Tarporley Hospital League of Friends is a charitable organisation that raises money for a local hospital. All of the members are volunteers.

Examples of internal information include:

- money raised at events
- charges for raffle tickets
- details of committee members.

Examples of external information include:

- charity regulations
- information on running raffles
- costs of venues for events
- needs of hospital for equipment
- interest rates
- details of donations and donors.

## TASK 6

For the tennis club example given earlier, and for the exams office, identify what is internal and external information.

The tennis club is only a small organisation and the exams office is just part (one function) of a much larger organisation, so imagine all of the different items of information required by a large organisation! That is why when we start to look at large organisations, we usually have to consider them as being made up of different sections, departments or functions – considering the whole organisation at once is too complex.

### Information flows

An information flow takes place when information moves from one place, or from one person, to another. Information can move in different ways. For example: in letters, reports, memos, documents of different types such as order forms, by word of mouth, in videos or via magazines. ICT is used to enable the flows of information to take place.

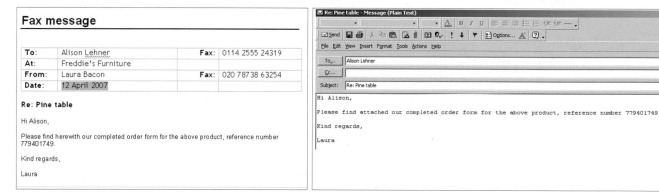

**Figure 2.6** Information flow – different ways to order a product

## TASK 7

1  Make a list of all of the different forms of information flow that are used in your school or college to provide you with information. Then consider how ICT is used to enable them to happen. Remember we don't use ICT for everything, some things are still better done manually. See:

http://www.telegraph.co.uk/news/main.jhtml?xml=/news/
     2006/08/04/ntext04.xml
http://www.out-law.com/page-4152
http://news.bbc.co.uk/2/hi/business/2949578.stm

2  Consider one of the organisations you have already looked at. Identify the ways the organisation uses to move information around. How is ICT used to enable this to happen?

### reminder

Understanding what makes good information will be important to you in every unit of this course that you study – after all that is the whole point of Information and Communications Technology!

### reminder

The purpose and people involved will determine the method of information flow. Whether or not ICT is used to enable it will be determined by the degree to which it makes the information flow more effective in some way than if ICT weren't used.

## In what form is information communicated?

When studying ICT it is easy to forget that not all information in organisations is communicated as written material. Some people find it easier to take in information given verbally, while others prefer it written down. Because organisations are made up of a range of individuals they have to use different forms of information for different purposes. As you may remember from earlier in the book (see page 14), good information is suited to its purpose and to the person who is using it. There is no point in verbally telling someone information that is going to be something that they need to keep referring to over a period of time. They will forget it. They need to have it in a written form. Some people find rows of figures very difficult to take in and prefer information shown as graphs or charts. Others find pictures or video useful.

So when you are looking at the information flows in the organisation that you are studying for your report, look at how it flows (the way or method used to transfer the information) and what form the information is in (pictures, numbers, text, graphs, spoken word, moving image, etc.). Make sure you understand why it is transferred using that particular method and form. Then look at how and why ICT is used to enable the information to flow and the form that it takes. Remember that the information would flow anyway, so why use ICT to enable it?

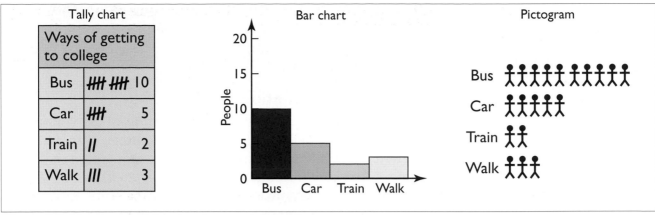

**Figure 2.7** Three ways of showing the same information

As you will discover, there are lots of methods of communicating information in different forms – visually, as written text, as still or moving pictures, numbers, diagrams or graphs; or orally in a meeting, a conversation or a telephone call. ICT can be used to enable all of these. ICT is not always the most effective method to use for communicating particular items of information. Think about what are the differences between having a telephone call and a face to face conversation. Why would you choose to use one rather than the other? Organisations are concerned with ensuring that the methods of communication they use are the most effective, so they will only use ICT where it is appropriate and the **best** method to employ.

## TASK 8

**I** Consider the following items of information and suggest what would be the best method for communicating the information. Use **Item 28** on the CD-ROM to record your answers.

**a)** Telling someone they are redundant.

**b)** A report for a sales manager to use when talking to clients.

**c)** Training materials on a new product that all branches of a multinational company need to know about.

**d)** Confirmation of an order made online.

**e)** A presentation on a design for a building by a firm of architects to their clients.

**f)** Figures on daily sales for a store manager.

Notice that the person/people as well as the information they need is being given. Why is this? Think back to what makes good information.

**2** Write down as many different ways of communicating information as you can think of.

When you are writing your report for your portfolio, one of the things that you have to include is the methods of communication used in the system/organisation on which you are writing the report. This is because, as mentioned below, one of the key things that ICT is used for is the transfer of information. You must emphasise what ICT methods are used and why they are used.

## Volumes of information

Notice that so far there has been no mention of the volume of information required by different organisations. This is a different issue. As the volumes (or amounts) increase so does the need for more formalised controls over the flows of information. The organisation's ICT infrastructure needs to be developed to accommodate greater flows of information and for the storage of data. For example, consider the volume of data being collected from every cash machine owned by one of the big banks, compared to the volume of data collected by the office of a small estate agents, in a day. Think about what the implications are for the ICT infrastructure as the volumes of data get bigger.

### TASK 9

1   Find out about any changes your school or college has had to make to the networks that it uses and the amount of data storage required by the school/college. Ask how and why the volumes of information have changed and/or how the networks have been altered over the past few years.

2   Find out about the volumes of data that will be involved in the identity card system that is being proposed or the National Health Service systems that are going to be introduced.

The volumes of data being moved around, and information being produced, can increase for many different reasons. These will be linked to changes in the size of an organisation as it expands physically – either in terms of the number of sites or personnel, or in terms of the volume or type of business done. A change to the form in which data are moved or information is produced, from largely text-based to visual forms, can lead to a dramatic increase in volumes of data.

**case study 7**

The BBC is an example of an organisation that has experienced a lot of change in the nature of its core business. Radio and TV used to be their traditional outlets for presenting current affairs, but the sources of information and the speed with which news stories are gathered has grown enormously, to the point where there are blogs dedicated to new stories. They also now have an enormous number of users going to their website for news, rather than to the television or radio.

## Task 10

Look at the size of different files containing pictures, both still and moving, or sounds, and compare them with files containing just words and numbers. What do you notice and how is this significant in terms of the flow and storage of information?

## ICT systems

### ICT systems are not just about PCs and mobiles!

It is important that you have a view of the type of systems and technologies used in organisations today. You will discover that not all organisations have the most up-to-date software, hardware or communications systems because every organisation has to justify what they want to buy. No organisation can afford to go out and buy the latest laptop or desktop, and certainly not the latest mainframe computer, unless they can justify that what the organisation will gain from it will far outweigh the cost of purchase. This is known as cost/benefit and is what should be considered as opposed to just the cost. The cost must be seen in the context of the gain that can be made from investing in the hardware and software.

This makes organisations quite different to individual ICT users who may purchase a new laptop just because it is the newest and most fashionable one to have or it has some new gadget with it. Individual users often don't consider the cost or the benefits they will get to the same degree as organisations!

## reminder

Because you are studying ICT at AS level you are expected to know the meaning of certain terms used in the ICT world. If you don't know what the terms mean then look at a reliable website, or an ICT/computing dictionary. The BCS Glossary referred to in **Item 5** on the CD-ROM is also a good starting point for ICT terms.

It is also worth having a look at an English dictionary if you find a word that you don't understand being used in this book.

Remember that when you come to doing the report in your portfolio for a strategic manager, you will have to make sure that **all** technical terms are explained, possibly making use of footnotes or a glossary.

 ## Getting down to the basics

When you start to do your research into an individual system or organisation, you need to start recording details. But you must not get overwhelmed by the detail or forget what it is you have got to demonstrate that you understand. The important thing is to remember just what ICT can do.

**ICT can help organisations to:**

- input
- store
- process
- transfer
- output information.

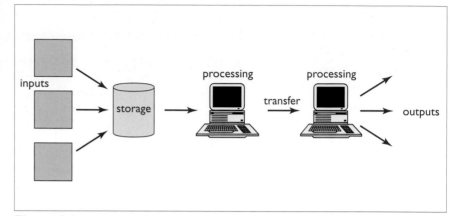

**Figure 2.8**

You can then identify how each of these activities is carried out and why it is done in the way it is. You will find it useful to remember the list above because it should help you to ask the right questions when you are doing your research.

You will be producing your report for **one** of the following:

- All the ICT systems used in an organisation (this would be a small enterprise)
- All the ICT systems used in one department within an organisation (medium or large enterprises)
- One ICT system that provides support to the whole organisation (medium or large enterprises).

To find out information about different sized enterprises, go to: http://www.sbs.gov.uk/SBS_Gov_files/researchandstats/SMESta ts2004.pdf.

You want to make sure that you will be able to understand what someone from the organisation may tell you, or at least be able to pretend that you do so you can go and look it up afterwards! And remember, don't get bogged down in lots of technical detail about the makes and models of hardware that they use, you are not interested in this detail, but in what it is used for and why.

You are given the choice of one of the above for your portfolio work because the size and complexity of organisations and the ICT systems used in them does vary tremendously. As a result, trying to study all of the ICT systems used to meet the needs of a whole organisation is only really appropriate if you are looking at a sole trader or small partnership (small enterprises) where the ICT systems mainly make use of a suite of generic software.

**Figure 2.9** Student interviewing someone in business

## TASK 11

There are many different 'types' of ICT system that you may come across when you do your research work for your portfolio. **Item 29** on the CD-ROM contains some references and questions to get you started on your research. The exam specification contains a list of the ones you should be able to identify, although so many ICT systems are now integrated that it is sometimes hard to tell where one ends and another begins, for example, stock control and sales systems in a supermarket.

### Effects of developments in ICT on working styles

Many people immediately think that the only thing that is affected by the introduction of ICT to an organisation is whether or not people lose their jobs. This is **not** what it is about! Notice that the specification says **working styles**.

Working styles encompasses the changes that have occurred in the way in which people do their jobs. Does ICT enable people to work in different places and in different ways? Do people now need to be more skilled in their jobs or do they just need different skills? Do people carry out the same activities but in different ways? For example, is using email rather than conventional (or snail) mail really any different? Do workers file documents electronically rather than putting pieces of paper in a filing cabinet? How are meetings held now? Do people visit one another or do they conference over the Internet or over special high-speed links? How do Blackberrys, PDAs and other new devices affect how people transfer information in their jobs?

## important note

It is really important that you understand what is meant by everything in this section of the book before you move on to the part about your portfolio. Students who jump into starting their portfolio without researching ICT systems first will definitely find it much harder to gain marks in the long run!

**Figure 2.10** Using ICT to work in different ways

## TASK 12

Interview some people who have seen changes in the way in which they work. A secretary and a manager would be suitable examples, or a salesman and a shop assistant. Remember they must be old enough to have experienced the changes that ICT systems have had on their working lives.

There is a form on the CD-ROM (**Item 30**) which you can use to help you.

## case study 8

**Figure 2.11** Car showroom

A car dealership had an ICT system installed to record information on sales, servicing and parts sold. The system was used on a number of workstations on a local area network within the dealership. The backup of the data in the system was designed to take place when all of the network stations were logged off. The people working at the dealership would arrive to start work at 8.30 in the morning to find that the system hadn't backed up because someone hadn't bothered to log off before they left work the evening before. This meant the staff then had to wait about half an hour to an hour while the backup was done before they could use the system, something that would never have happened before the system was automated. The solution was to make one person responsible for ensuring that the backup had taken place. That member of staff had to start work at 8.00 a.m. in order that the backup was completed before everyone else arrived. Working style was affected for one member of staff to stop it being affected for every other member of staff.

Was this a well-designed system? No – because it did not take into account the way in which the staff worked. The designers of the system did not think about the need for all of the staff to log off at the end of a day as the only trigger for the backup. It could be argued that the system was good but that the training given in how to use it wasn't, because the staff did not realise the implications of not logging off. What is interesting is the way round the problem that was adopted by the company!

# Skills you will need for this unit

## Research

▶ The first thing that most students do when asked to research something is to get on the Internet and do a search! This is not the only way to find out about organisations. At this level of study, you are expected to be able to research using lots of different resources. One of the most important things that you can do is talk to people. There will be many different organisations in your local area. Start by making yourself a list of all the organisations that you come into contact with every day. Then think about what their purpose is and what type of organisation they are. You will be surprised at just how many organisations you have contact with on a day-to-day basis.

The table opposite shows some of the contacts the author of this book had on one day – well one morning!

**Figure 2.12**

| Organisation | What for |
|---|---|
| Local dairy | Milk delivery |
| Newsagents | Paper delivery |
| Post office | Post delivery |
| Northern writers group | Letter requesting renewal of membership in post – there are lots of other organisations that could have been included here! |
| Grocery company | Neighbour's home delivery vehicle blocks lane! |
| Taxi firm | Taxi to station |
| Railway company | Train to work |
| Bus company | Transport to meeting |
| Company XYZ and ABC | Meeting with representatives from these companies |
| And by now it is only 9.00 a.m. !! | |

## reminder

Many of what were called 'public utility' companies are no longer public companies – they are private, profit-making organisations. So be careful, if you choose one of these you must also study another organisation that is public.

Having tried to list organisations that you have contact with, decide what type of organisation each one is. Taking the example in the table above, most of these are either large or small commercial organisations and there is one charitable one. Can you group the ones in the table into these categories?

With your own list of organisations, think about what different types of organisation they are, and about which ones you could most easily find out more. Who could you talk to? Which ones might have published information about themselves? All large organisations produce some sort of annual report. For limited companies and plcs this is a legal requirement. All charitable organisations have to have some sort of annual meeting where there are details given out about what the organisation has achieved during the year. Also, they all have constitutions that describe how they are managed. These documents won't tell you specifically about the ICT used by the organisations but they will tell you about:

- different sizes and types of organisation
- their purposes
- their information handling needs (in terms of what information they need, what they need it for and how they use it).

If an organisation is a small and local one, you can probably find out what ICT systems they use and why they use them, by talking to someone. Large public organisations often have details about their ICT systems that they provide to customers or suppliers. For example, doctors receive details of the ICT systems used by the NHS that they have to know about. Individuals can also find out about ICT systems used by, for example, the DVLA, by visiting their website and seeing what

**Figure 2.13** Garage

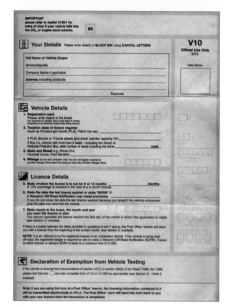

**Figure 2.14** Car tax renewal form that can be scanned at a post office

## reminder

Some of the references given in **Item 29** on the CD-ROM are to websites of manufacturers where case studies are given. Also try companies like IBM UK, Hewlett Packard and Surf Control.

is available there, or talking to a mechanic who does MOTs or visiting a post office where car tax disks are issued. Companies that launch their services online often send out material to customers explaining what they are doing and why. For example, when bills or bank statements are changed, customers are notified.

Other useful sources of information are the websites of companies that supply ICT systems to organisations. These often give examples of where their systems are used and for what purpose.

Other places to look for information are in business magazines. This website: http://www.uknetguide.co.uk/Business/Business_Services/Business_Publications.html provides, among other things, links to different magazines – some general and some on specific business areas. Another website that provides a list of links to magazines to do with computing is: http://www.wrx.zen.co.uk/magazines.htm.

Also, the National Computing Centre produces a magazine called *CIOConnect* for 'The IT leaders of today and tomorrow'.

There are magazines/newspapers like the *Farmers Guardian* or *Farmers Weekly*, aimed at agriculture, and *Accounting Today*, all of which often contain articles about the use of ICT in different organisations. You can even find articles about how ICT is used and why, in magazines on planes or trains.

Another valuable resource that provides very up-to-date information is newspapers. There may be some articles that you can read, even in your local paper. Websites such as those for some of the main daily newspapers, (http://www.guardian.co.uk/, http://www.telegraph.co.uk/ and http://www.timesonline.co.uk/uk/) provide facilities for searching for information from back copies of newspapers.

Hopefully, you now have an idea of some of the various sources of information available for your research and you won't just rely on copying the contents of one website for one organisation, which you then put in your portfolio as evidence for the section on research! This isn't the way to obtain maximum marks. If you have been and looked at some of the websites referred to in **Item 29** on the CD-ROM you will realise that you can obtain information from lots of different sources. It is just a question of looking in different places until you find what you want.

## Report writing

For Unit 1 you had to produce either a newsletter or a set of web pages, which displayed information in the most appropriate way for a particular audience and purpose. For this unit you have to produce a formal report. Your audience is a strategic manager who is not an ICT specialist.

## So what is a formal report?

A formal report is information displayed in a logical and organised format. It is factual in nature, clear and easily understood by the person/people it is produced for. Reports are used very frequently in organisations and it is likely that you will have to write them yourself at some stage in your future career. If you go on to further or higher education you will most likely have to produce a dissertation on a subject – again as a formal report and with a similar structure.

To understand what a formal report should look like, have a look at some websites where there are formal reports published or get hold of some copies of reports. Don't worry about understanding the content, what you should look at is:

- the structure
- the way diagrams, charts and figures are used
- the way in which information sources are referenced
- lists of figures, tables, maps, diagrams, headings and side headings
- how quotes from people are shown
- how the author and content of quoted material is acknowledged
- how diagrams are captioned and whether the source of the diagram is given
- whether graphs have scales shown on them.

For an example of a well-presented company report go to: http://www2.marksandspencer.com/thecompany/investor relations/annual_review06/downloads/index.shtml.
The Reuters website also has company reports you can view at: http://today.reuters.com/business/companyprofiles.aspx.

Remember always to be critical of what you read and try to understand what makes a report good or bad – in other words what is good or poor quality information and whether ICT has been used effectively to create the information. So look at how the information is displayed and then think about what software functions can be used to achieve it.

There are lots of examples of formal reports around. Look at the government stationery office site for past government reports; these are usually very formal and hard to read! Company reports designed for shareholders can provide good ideas for reports

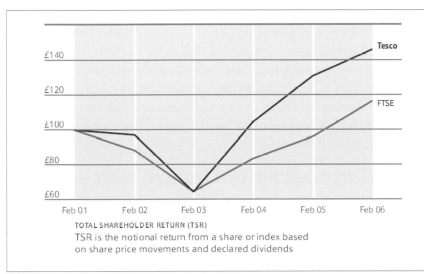

TOTAL SHAREHOLDER RETURN (TSR)
TSR is the notional return from a share or index based on share price movements and declared dividends

**Figure 2.15** Extract from a company report

suitable for the general public. Have a look for some companies that you know of, or organisations that you belong to, and see whether you can find any reports that they have produced, or choose something that interests you and do an Internet search for relevant reports. University and college websites often have guidance on writing reports on research work and dissertations. The QCA (Qualifications and Curriculum Authority) and JCQ (Joint Council for Qualifications), BECTA (British Educational, Communications and Technology Agency), DEFRA (Department for the Environment, Food and Rural Affairs) all have lots of reports that are available to download from their websites.

 **Item 31** on the CD-ROM is an example of a formal report. The report that you produce should have the following:

- A title page, containing report title, author's name, date and course title.
- A contents page, with title, listing the sections of the report.
- An introduction, stating the purpose of the report and how the information it contains was obtained.
- The main body of the report, broken into logical sections, each with a clear heading or sub-heading. Each paragraph should contain factual information that is discussed or explained. Paragraphs may be numbered systematically. Captioned diagrams, tables and illustrations may be included at appropriate points in the text.
- Reference may be made to appendices, but don't use them if you don't need to as people rarely read them.
- A conclusion or summary, that sums up the main findings.
- A list of resources used.
- An index listing references to key words in the text.
- Page numbers.
- Consistent styles for headings and sub-headings and all text.
- Headers and footers.
- Content referenced using footnotes or endnotes.

Remember, as well, that the quality of the written communication you use is assessed in your work. The style of writing should be appropriate for the reader.

You must remember that the person reading the report is not a technical ICT specialist and so the use of abbreviations or technical terms that are not explained should be avoided.

A report of this type should be checked carefully for spelling and grammatical errors!

## Producing diagrams of inputs, processes and outputs

There are various ways in which you can document the flow of information around an organisation, and the inputs and outputs to a system. There are many textbooks available on

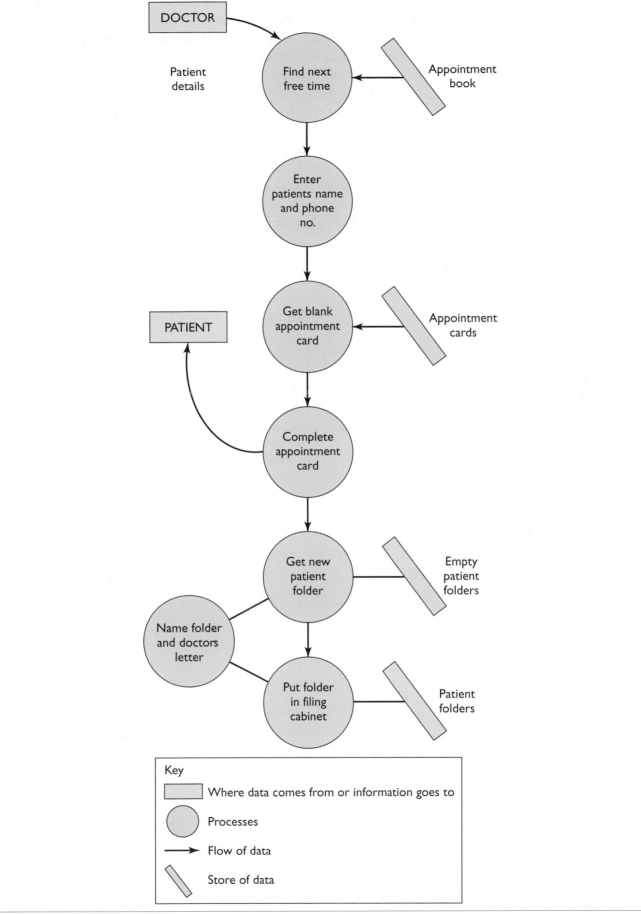

**Figure 2.16** Sample diagram showing inputs, outputs and processes

information systems that show techniques for doing this, or your teacher may show you several different ways. **Items 33a–d** on the CD-ROM contain some example diagrams.

There is no requirement for you to use any particular method for producing diagrams to show information flows, so long as you remember to include a key so that other people can understand them. They are useful because they can show very simply what would otherwise require a lot of words. Diagrams are also useful for checking with people from the organisation that you have got things right. If you are doing the full double award and are going to be studying Unit 13 on Systems Analysis, now is a good time to start trying out some of the techniques you will need for this.

## Software skills

The skills that you can demonstrate in using the functionality of a piece of software are assessed under the A01 Assessment Objective. For this unit, part of your portfolio is a formal report, and the software functions that you need to show you can use are those that are appropriate for producing a formal report. What you are expected to produce is described above so you should be practising the functions needed to create the features that you need to include. The following list gives some examples of these features:

- automated page numbering
- creating section breaks to enable the correct pagination of the report, or using widow and orphan control
- creating headers and footers (including different ones for different sections)
- automatic creation of a table of contents
- creating, or customising, paragraph styles in order to add impact to the report
- automatic creation of an index with multiple page references, where appropriate
- inserting footnotes and/or endnotes to references and abbreviations used
- inserting captions or numbered labels.

Try to make sure that you can do all of these things before you start your formal report itself. The reason being that it is much better and easier to set these up when you first start on a document than when you are halfway through writing it! You should be able to find examples of all of these features in this book.

Remember also to try out things like producing a customised dictionary and ensure that you are using a UK dictionary for spellchecking!

# The portfolio

► For this unit you have to complete a portfolio of work. This has three main parts to it:

1. Research work that demonstrates your understanding of how and why organisations use ICT, and the effect that the size and type of organisation has on information-handling needs.
2. A detailed report written for a senior manager who is a non-ICT specialist, on **either**:
   ■ one small organisation and all of the ICT systems used **or**
   ■ one large department and the ICT systems it uses **or**
   ■ one ICT system and how it is used by the whole of a large organisation.
3. The common elements for all portfolios, such as planning, evaluation, written communication and standard ways of working.

## Planning

This falls under the third part but needs to be done first! When you are planning your work, make sure that you have a clear understanding of what you have got to do in the time available. You need to make sure that you leave sufficient time for things to perhaps not go quite as you imagine they will. Leaving a little spare time at the end of the period of time that your teacher has given you to complete the work would be sensible, just in case you have any problems.

The record should show where you got behind or in front of your time plan and how you adjusted it to take account of delays or spent the extra time you found you had.

Be honest! The exam board is looking to see whether you have learnt from what you have done. For example, many students often underestimate how long it takes to find the information for their research section, or to make contact with their 'client' to check the report contents for accuracy.

Unlike Unit 1 there is no split into investigation time and controlled conditions and so it is even more important that you plan your time carefully yourself. It may be that your teacher gives you some interim deadlines to help you, or it may be left entirely up to you, in which case you must definitely try not to leave things to the last minute. Work at this standard cannot be rushed over a weekend or done the night before. There is just too much to do and you need to give yourself the chance to look back at work already completed and improve it.

> ## reminder
>
> If you look at the examination board website you will probably find the date that the board expects the marks to be in for portfolio work. It is no use thinking that you have got all of the time up to then as the marks have to arrive by that date and your teacher will have all of their marking and administration to do before they can send off the marks. So listen to the date that the teacher gives you!

Here is a quote from the Principal Moderator's report from June 2006:

… candidates need to produce some kind of time plan, showing how they intend to use their time in order to produce their portfolio of evidence. This may be combined with the evidence which describes the actions that they need to take to produce the portfolio of evidence (referred to as 'the problem'). To gain the higher marks the candidate should include not only an estimated time of completion for each action planned, but should update this at frequent intervals to show that they are monitoring their progress and making any necessary adjustments. They will gain maximum marks if they can explain why any deadlines have been missed and what action has been taken to get back on track for the final deadline. Perfect time planning is not expected of candidates at this stage of their learning and it is far better for candidates to be honest than to pretend that everything has gone to schedule.

AQA Chair of Examiners Report Applied ICT June 2006

You have to be able to produce:

- a plan for the work to be done showing what needs to be carried out, the sequence of activities and an estimation of the time involved
- a record to show whether this plan was followed and any adjustments that were made in order to complete the tasks.

This table is a section taken from the marking grid that your teacher will almost certainly use to assess your work:

| I mark | 2 marks | 3 marks | 4 marks |
|--------|---------|---------|---------|
| Candidate has provided a brief description of actions taken to solve the problem. | Candidate has described actions taken to solve the problem. | Candidate has clearly described actions taken to solve the problem and shown a clear understanding of what they have done and why. | Candidate has clearly described actions taken to solve the problem and demonstrated a clear understanding of what they have done and why. Candidate has also shown clearly how changes made have improved their portfolio. |
| Candidate has provided limited evidence of time management or planning. | Candidate has provided some evidence of time management and planning. They have met some deadlines and have shown that they understand the need to monitor their progress. | Candidate has provided strong evidence of time management and planning, fully monitored their progress and met deadlines. Reasons for any missed deadlines have been explained. | |

If you have already completed Unit 1 and been examined on this, how did you get on? Was time planning a weak area that you could improve on? If you look at the marking grid that your teacher may use to assess your work you will see that there are three marks for the time planning and also four marks for describing the actions that you took to 'solve the problem'. In this case your 'problem' is producing the portfolio and so you need to describe what you did in order to complete the work, as well as when and why.

The following is a list of some of the things you might need to start with doing to produce your portfolio:

- Read up in a textbook about what you need to do for this unit and make a time plan.
- List all the organisations you have contact with and decide which might be suitable for your research.
- Investigate organisation 'X'. Go to the library and also do Internet searches.
- Investigate organisation 'Y'. Go to the library and also do Internet searches.
- Organise interview with Mr Jones from 'X'.
- Go and interview Mr Jones.
- Write up interview notes and send them to him for confirmation.

This is just the start of all the things you need to do. There are also other things that you may be doing at the same time as these, for example, finding out what formal reports look like and what they should contain for the second part of your portfolio, and learning about the software functions that you will need to use for the report.

This really is the only time Gantt charts are useful in portfolios – for when you want to show how several different activities will overlap in terms of the time that is needed for them.

If you look back at the example of part of a time plan given in Section 1 on page 36, this will give you ideas for producing your own. Also, **Item 34** on the CD-ROM is a freeware program, 'Gantt Project', which you may find useful for your planning.

## Part I The general research

The research section of the report helps you to gain marks for the Assessment Objectives 2 and 3 (A02 and A03). In other words, what is being looked for is evidence of your understanding of the role of ICT systems in organisations and your ability to be able to draw conclusions from information that you have researched. It is not about simply including lots of facts about different organisations that you have copied from web pages!

**definition**

**Gantt chart**
Gantt chart is a popular type of bar that illustrates a project schedule. Named after Henry L Gantt.

**reminder**

It is most important that you understand what is meant by plagiarism. You must read the advice for candidates provided by the JCQ, because if you do commit plagiarism then you can be disqualified from the examination! See:
http://www.jcq.org.uk/attachments/published/277/1/6.%20Notice%20to%20Candidates%20Coursework%20FINAL%202006.pdf
This is also included as **Item 36** on the CD-ROM.

**definition**

**Moderators**
Moderators are the people employed by the examination board to check that the standard of marking at your centre is the same as everywhere else in the country.

If you have read the earlier parts of this section then you should now understand what ICT can do for organisations, what is meant by different types of organisations and how ICT is used to meet the information handling needs of different organisations.

What you have to include is:

- evidence of research into different types of organisations and their different information handling needs. This will cover:
  – different sizes and types of organisations
  – their purposes
  – their information handling needs
  – different types of ICT systems.

What you have to remember is that:

- you must use several sources of research – not just the Internet
- you must state all sources of research used
- you must not just include copies of articles or web pages
- you must write things in your own words to be able to show your understanding
- more does not mean a better mark – quite often in this section it means the opposite.

Moderators and teachers do get very fed up with portfolios that include pages of material, for this part of the work, where absolutely no marks can be awarded because students have not remembered these points! What they want to see is a clear understanding shown by students.

Things to notice from the marking grid opposite that apply to this section of the portfolio are:

- You must make sure that you include information about at least two different ICT systems.
- These must be for at least two different types and sizes of organisation, for example, the personnel system in a large public organisation and a stock control system in a small private organisation. (Look carefully at the bits in bold in the table.)
- Make sure that you name the organisations that you are using to illustrate your findings and state what type of organisation they are.
- The examples that you use should be helping you to be able to complete the third row – explaining how ICT helps organisations to fulfil their purposes. Do not get involved in too much detail – it is all about why and how organisations use ICT and the differences that size and type of organisation make and **not** about all of the different items of hardware that they have.

| 1 mark | 2 marks | 3 marks |
|---|---|---|
| In their research the candidate has briefly described the role of at least one ICT system in an organisation. | In their research the candidate has described, in some detail, the role of at least one ICT system in an organisation. | |
| In their research the candidate has briefly described the role of at least one ICT system (of a **different type** from the system above) in an organisation of a **different type and size**. | In their research the candidate has described, in some detail, the role of at least one ICT system (of a **different type** from the system above) in an organisation of a **different type and size**. | |
| In their research, the candidate has provided a basic description of how ICT systems used by organisations help them to meet their data handling needs. | In their research, the candidate has provided a detailed description of how ICT systems used by organisations help them to meet their data handling needs. | In their research, the candidate has provided a detailed description of how ICT systems used by organisations help them to meet their data handling needs by explaining these in terms of the organisations' purposes. |
| Candidate has listed the information sources used for their research. | Candidate has stated what information was selected from each source listed, for use in their research. | Candidate has explained why the information selected was appropriate for use in their research. |

- The last row is looking at your ability to use different research sources, to record these correctly and to assess what information you use from which sources and why – reasons could be things like reliability, or being the most up-to-date information.

## Part 2  The formal report

You will need to produce the following:

- A formal report that contains details of:
  - how one specific ICT system in an organisation handles information in a way that meets the organisation's needs
  - diagrams and descriptions of the input, processing and output for that system
  - the effect of ICT on working styles within the organisation.

- The report should include all of the elements of a formal report that are given in the section on reports on page 78.
- Evaluation criteria for the report.
- An annotated draft report, showing where amendments are required to the structure and layout and content of the report.

The formal report is the part of the portfolio that carries the most marks. Some of these marks are for your appropriate use of the software to create the report, some for the research that you have done to produce it, some for the content and some for the way that you have produced and edited the report. Marks gained on the formal report are awarded against assessment objectives A01, A02 and A03 and, for the evaluation criteria, under A04.

As mentioned previously, the report that you write should be based on:

- one small organisation and all of its information handling needs **or**
- one large department and its information handling needs **or**
- one ICT system and how it is used to meet the information handling needs of a large organisation.

So, for example, your report could be on the information handling needs of a small painting and decorating company, or the use an intranet is put to in a company, or the information handling needs of the personnel department of a major chain store.

It is important to try to find an organisation yourself about which you can write the report. Ideally this should be an organisation where you have a contact who could introduce you to someone else to speak to, if they themselves do not have the information that you need. It is always much easier to do work for something that is real rather than something that is made up. Certainly the students who produce reports on real organisations generally gain the better marks. Your teacher should be able to help you, but look back at all of the organisations with which you have contact and have listed – see pages 74–5.

The principal moderator's report from 2006 June said:

Candidates who had the involvement of a real client had a clearer idea of what was required than those who did not ... Where candidates had engaged with a real client the portfolio of work often had a narrower focus with the candidate having a clearer idea of how what they produced was meeting the needs stated. This tended to make it easier for those candidates to access the higher marks.

AQA Chair of Examiners Report Applied ICT June 2006

## Who the report is for

You should try to write your report for a 'strategic manager who is a non-ICT specialist'. So what does that mean? Look back on page 65 where there was a description of what is meant by 'strategic' in an ICT context and think about the implications of the reader not being an ICT specialist. This means that you will have to make sure that all technical terms are explained and that you don't use abbreviations that you are familiar with, but that they may not be.

---

### TASK 13

1   What do the following stand for?
    **a**  CD-ROM
    **b**  MIPS
    **c**  VGA
    **d**  HTML
    **e**  ASCII
    **f**  DVD
2   What do the following terms mean?
    **a**  ergonomic
    **b**  real time
    **c**  batch processing
    **d**  synchronous
    **e**  reciprocity

---

It may be that your teacher will suggest the sort of person the report is to be written for – such as a new member of staff, a bank manager the organisation wants to obtain finance from, or a possible investor.

It is important to establish who you are aiming the report at before you start to write it because this will affect the style and content of the report and the evaluation criteria and subsequent testing. A report could be written for the senior manager in a particular business area, for example marketing, who wants to know how the department is using ICT at the moment and what services it provides for his department. This is fairly typical information for a department head to want to know, particularly if they are relatively new in a job. This is because it gives them information on which they can base future decisions. Reports are often used as the basis for decision making and for this reason it is important that the information that they contain is factually correct.

Another typical use of this type of report would be for decision making at a board of directors level. The scenario could be that ICT systems are in use more in certain departments than others and the board wants to know how a particular department is making use of ICT to determine future spending. Alternatively, it could be to provide

1. Your contact with a client (person for whom the report is being written or who has commissioned the report) does not have to be face-to-face. You can exchange information using lots of different methods, as you should already have found out!

2. Make sure that contact with people is referenced in your report and that there is clear evidence of meetings, etc. by getting things signed off, using email evidence and so on – this is the sort of thing that can go in the third section of the portfolio.

information for new employees. If it is a small organisation that is being reported on then the information may help the owner or chairperson to decide on the future use of ICT. One thing that is important is that the report should be factual. There is no requirement for you to be critical of the ICT systems that the company uses. You just need to be able to explain what they use and why, as well as what benefits it gives to the business.

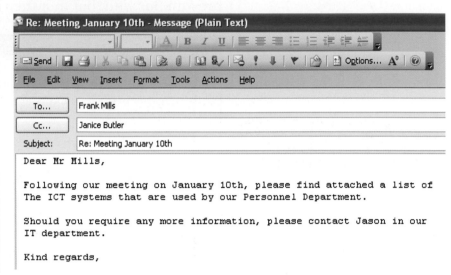

**Figure 2.17** Example of an email that could be included in your work to show contact that you have with your client

### Evaluation criteria

You will notice in the list earlier (see pages 85–6) that you are expected to produce evaluation criteria for the report. You can only produce your evaluation criteria after you have established who the report is going to be produced for, its purpose, and what the people who are going to need to read it are like. This is so that you can select the most appropriate style and means of showing the information, for example, using graphs and charts rather than tables of figures, or diagrams rather than words. This is a lot easier for a formal report because they tend to have very standard features – see the earlier section on reports on pages 77–8.

The evaluation criteria are statements about what your solution (the report) should be like, what it should contain and how the information should be presented. These criteria are what you should test your draft report against and what you will use to assess the success or otherwise of your final report in your evaluation.

They should **not** be a list of requirements or of the bits that you have got to make or do. The following table shows some examples of what **are** or **are not** acceptable as typical criteria.

| Not acceptable | Acceptable |
|---|---|
| The report should include headers and footers. | The report should be no longer than 15 A4 pages, nor contain more than 5,000 words. |
| The report should have section headings. | The structure of the report should make it easy for the reader to find the information that they want. |
| There should be pictures included. | Suitable diagrams or pictures that do not infringe any copyright should be included where they are needed to illustrate the text. |

**reminder**

Qualitative criteria are based on opinions and quantitative criteria can be measured. Which of the acceptable criteria in the table above is quantitative and which are qualitative?

One thing that is worth thinking about when you write your evaluation criteria is how you are going to test your report against these criteria. This will affect not only the marks for the criteria and testing, but also the quality of your evaluation.

If you produce criteria like the ones on the left of the table and simply test the report by reading it yourself and making comments, you will be lucky to gain even one mark. If you have a clear idea of the purpose of the report and who it is being written for, and you understand the difference between qualitative and quantitative evaluation criteria, and how the report should be tested against these, then you should be able to get three marks. (Look at the marking grid on page 96 in the section on evaluation of the solution.)

## Assessing the research for the report

The following table shows what you need to provide evidence of in order to gain marks for the research that you carry out in relation to the organisation/system for the report and who the report is written for.

| 1 mark | 2 marks | 3 marks |
|---|---|---|
| Candidate has listed the information sources used for their research for their final report. | Candidate has stated what information was selected, from each source listed, for use in their final report. | Candidate has explained why the information selected was appropriate for use in their final report. |
| Candidate has produced a report that provides limited evidence of research into the organisation, for whom the report has been written, and its purposes. | Candidate has produced a report that provides much evidence of research into the organisation, for whom the report has been written, and its purposes. | |
| Candidate has produced a report that provides limited evidence of research into how the organisation makes use of information to support its purposes. | Candidate has produced a report that provides much evidence of research into how the organisation makes use of information to support its purposes. | Candidate has produced a report that provides detailed evidence of research into how the organisation makes use of information to support its purposes. |

It is important that you do think about these in advance as these marks are for what you have to **do**, not what you produce. The hard bit is to provide the evidence that you have done it.

The first row is something that is fairly straightforward because you should be able to list the research sources you have used. Do remember that this includes people as well as reports, books or websites. It would also include things like work shadowing, observing people at work, or studying sample documents. As stated for the research section, the difference between gaining one and three marks depends on whether you have said what information you have used from each source and why it was appropriate to use it.

The content of the second row of the table relates to making sure you have all the information that you need about who the report is for and what its purpose is.

The third row of the table refers to the investigation and research that you have actually done. If you have done no more than one interview and nothing else, then do not expect to gain high marks here! However, there are lots of techniques that you can use if you have a real client for the report and a real organisation that you can investigate.

## Assessment of the report

The table opposite shows how the content of your report will be assessed.

## Background

Row 1 in the opposite is seeking to assess whether it is possible to understand who the organisation is that you are writing about and what they do. Remember that you could be writing about a whole organisation, a department, or about one ICT system across all departments. Exactly what is relevant to include will depend on who and what the report is for. Do remember that even if it is for someone who already works for the organisation it may also need to be shown to someone from outside the organisation and that the background section should provide the 'scope' of the report.

The person reading the report should have a clear understanding of what the organisation does, what type of organisation it is, the size of the organisation, its geographical spread and the way it is organised.

This is where things like organisation charts are useful because they can show things very clearly and you can identify the department or areas the report will be concerned with – though don't think that this is all you need to include!

## reminder

The scope of the report gives the areas and issues that are to be covered by the report. It should indicate what system(s) or departments are to be included. Look out for this in any reports that you study. Sometimes this is done by including a summary at the start of the report.

| 1 mark | 2 marks | 3 marks | 4 marks |
|---|---|---|---|
| In their report the candidate has provided some background information about the organisation. | In their report the candidate has provided detailed background information about the organisation. | | |
| In their report the candidate has provided a basic description of the information needs of a specific organisation. | In their report the candidate has described how one specific ICT system handles the needs of a specific organisation. | In their report the candidate has described how one specific ICT system handles the needs of a specific organisation. The candidate has referred in detail to its inputs, outputs and the methods of communication used. | In their report the candidate has also explained the way that the specific system helps the organisation to meet its purpose and goals. |
| In their report the candidate has provided a basic description of the processing taking place within the system. | In their report the candidate has provided a detailed description of the processing taking place within the system. | | |
| In their report the candidate has provided a statement about how ICT has had an effect on working styles within the organisation. | In their report the candidate has provided a detailed description about how ICT has had an effect on working styles within the organisation. | In their report the candidate has provided a detailed description that explains how ICT has affected working styles within the organisation. | |

## Describing inputs, processes and outputs

In the second and third rows of the table, the assessment is concerned with whether you understand the system(s) that you are writing about. Can you identify the inputs needed for the system? What are they and where do they come from? How are they obtained? What happens to the inputs in the system and how do they get converted into the outputs or what the system has to produce?

Often it is much easier to start with what is produced by a system and then work backwards to find out what is needed to produce it.

An example would be if you were looking at the use of an intranet in a company. Identify first what the intranet is used for and who it is used by. It could be that the personnel department use it to inform staff members of events that are happening, reminders about health and safety issues or sporting events to which trips are being organised. It could be that the production department use it to inform people of the shifts they are working the following week or the number of hours they have worked, changes in teams, and so on. These are the uses and outputs. Where does the input information come from? Who provides it? Who formats the information and puts it onto the intranet (processing)?

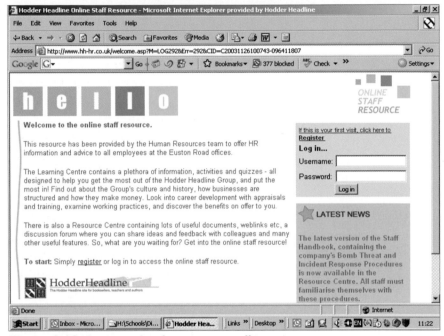

**Figure 2.18** An example of a company staff intranet

For a stock control system the purpose would be to make sure that there is always stock in the store, there are no inaccuracies in stock values, there is no wastage, the amount of money spent on stock is minimised to obtain a better profit margin, and customers do not have to wait for items, meaning that they keep using the store.

The outputs will be things like reordering lists for individual suppliers, stock lists for managers, turnover reports for senior management and query reports for items in stock for staff and customers. The inputs will be supplier details, stock details (like minimum quantities or turnover rates) and warehouse details, etc. Processing will require searching the stock database, matching the amount in stock with reorder quantities and basically whatever else is required to produce the outputs.

Understanding about different types of systems used in organisations will allow you to ask the right questions of representatives of the organisation.

**Figure 2.19** Supermarket stockroom

Notice that for the highest marks you must have 'explained the way that the specific system helps the organisation to meet its purpose and goals'. Looking at the previous paragraphs, can you see any descriptions of the organisation's purpose and goals? Where would you describe these? They should go in the background for the whole organisation and then the role of the system(s) you are looking at should be described. Everything else is then dedicated to explaining how these are achieved.

### Working styles

The last row in the table on page 91, concerned with the content of the report, is assessing your understanding of the effect on working styles in the organisation. Make sure that you think about how you are going to get this information and who you would need to speak to. The difference in the marks you can get is based on whether you have stated, described or explained effects on working styles. If you don't talk about the organisation the report is for, you will get no marks for this.

### The report – or marks for A01 Practical capability in using ICT

The table on page 94 includes all of the things that are awarded marks under the heading of A01 – Practical capability. They are about the construction of your report and the use of functions available in the software. They also include elements of testing and error correction.

When you are producing your report you should print out a first draft, which you can then annotate to show the corrections that you need to make to it. You should show corrections that are needed to the structure and layout in addition to any errors you have made when entering data into the report layout. (See rows 1 and 2 in the following table.)

Row 1 of the table is concerned with things that you may want to correct, such as the layouts of paragraphs or tables, where they become split over a page break and the arrangement of diagrams or charts within the report so that they are close to where they are referred to in the writing. It may be that you decide that the order of the sections isn't logical and you want to move them around, or that you have used the wrong style for some of the headings.

The criteria in Row 2 of the table are looking for you to have checked the actual wording for correctness. As mentioned previously (page 78) a spellchecker does not pick up the incorrect use of a word or some spelling errors. Grammar checkers may not pick up the meaning that you intended. This means that it is actually necessary to check yourself for this

| 1 mark | 2 marks | 3 marks |
|---|---|---|
| Candidate has produced an initial draft of the report. | Candidate has produced an initial draft of the report and annotated it to show changes to structure and layout. | Candidate has produced corrected final version of the report that incorporates the changes, in addition to the annotated draft. |
| Candidate has proofread the report and annotated errors requiring correction. | Candidate has proofread the report and annotated errors requiring correction that can be easily understood. | Candidate has proofread the report and annotated errors requiring correction that can be easily understood. Candidate has also produced a final version of the report that is free from obvious errors. |
| Candidate has produced a report that has little structure. | Candidate has produced a report that has a formal structure and is divided into logical sections. | Candidate has produced a highly structured report with appropriate, numbered sections and paragraphs. |
| Candidate has produced a report that uses a header/footer. | Candidate has produced a report that uses a header/footer that identifies the report content and author. | Candidate has produced a report that uses a header/footer that identifies the report content and author and reflects the section headings. |
| Candidate has produced a report that has a basic index. | Candidate has produced a report containing an index that references some appropriate key words. | Candidate has produced a report containing an index that comprehensively references appropriate key words. |
| Candidate has produced a report that incorporates diagrams and/or other illustrations. | Candidate has produced a report that incorporates diagrams and/or other illustrations that are referenced using captions. | |
| Candidate has produced a report that uses footnotes and/or endnotes. | Candidate has produced a report that uses footnotes and/or endnotes appropriately. | |
| Candidate has produced a statement about copyright in relation to the report. | Candidate has stated what actions have been taken to ensure that the report fully complies with copyright. | |

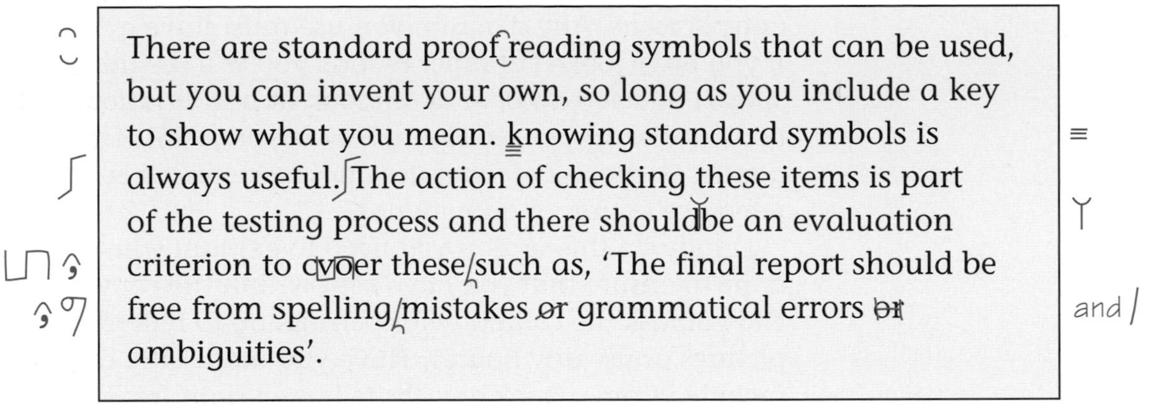

There are standard proofreading symbols that can be used, but you can invent your own, so long as you include a key to show what you mean. knowing standard symbols is always useful. The action of checking these items is part of the testing process and there should be an evaluation criterion to cover these, such as, 'The final report should be free from spelling mistakes or grammatical errors or ambiguities'.

*and* /

**Figure 2.20** Example of proofreading marks

**reminder**

You only need to include **one** draft copy and the final copy of the report – putting in three or four draft copies will gain no extra marks – and **do** remember to check that you have corrected any errors in the final report. If you don't, you will lose easy marks!

---

**TASK 14**

1 Find out what an ambiguity is.
2 Find out what is meant by the phrase 'errors and omissions excepted' and when it is used – hopefully you will not need to use it in your report!

---

**reminder**

The page numbering for the report must be different from the rest of the portfolio. The report should be a stand-alone document.

---

sort of error by reading through and marking up the draft copy where there are errors. This is called proofreading and it is something that is checked and rechecked when writing a book! You may need to get your teacher to confirm that you have done this. There are standard proofreading symbols that can be used, but you can invent your own, so long as you include a key to show what you mean. Knowing standard symbols is always useful. The following URL is the website of the British Standards Institution, who publish official marks for copy preparation and proof correction: www.bsi-uk.com.

The action of checking these items is part of the testing process and there should be an evaluation criterion to cover these, such as, 'The final report should be free from spelling mistakes, grammatical errors and ambiguities'.

Rows 3, 4 and 5 of the table are about you using software functions effectively and correctly. Use heading styles and a consistent, logical layout. Use the software to produce a header on each page detailing what the report is about: **not** 'ICT2 portfolio', but something like 'Report on the use of the company intranet at XYZ industries, prepared by P. Ralph, March 2007'. Make sure that the header/footer is used to identify the different sections of the report. This is something that is particularly useful if you are flicking through trying to find a particular topic.

Ensure that you prepare an index (note that this is not the same as a list of contents). Look at this book, or some reports, to see what this is and how it works. To produce the index you are expected to use the functions available within the software that you use to produce the report. The fact that you've used the functions in the software may need to be confirmed by your teacher because a reader cannot tell from the printed copy.

Row 6 is about using pictures/diagrams or graphs and tables of figures to explain things. You might, for example, include an information flow chart, a decomposition diagram or a data flow diagram. You might include photographs of an office environment or a data capture device, or screenshots of data entry screens. Any diagram you use must have a caption and if you have looked at other reports you will see how these should be referenced, or again look at how it is done in this book (for example, see Figure 2.20 on page 95). The same applies to the use of footnotes and endnotes, often used to reference figures or quotations.

Finally, in this section you need to explain what you have done to ensure that you have kept within the copyright law. Did you ask the company for permission to reproduce any pictures or use any figures? Have you made sure that anything included from a book or website is copyright free or in the public domain?

## Part 3

This relates to the general aspects of the portfolio that are common to all portfolio work. It also includes the planning aspects, dealt with on page 81. This is where you have to describe any problems and the actions/changes you had to take/make as a result. The marking for this is shown on page 82.

This table shows the marks for evaluation criteria and testing and for the evaluation of the solution – the report:

| 1 mark | 2 marks | 3 marks |
|---|---|---|
| Candidate has provided some evaluation criteria for the solution (report) and has carried out some testing. | Candidate has provided both qualitative and quantitative evaluation criteria, some of which are appropriate to assess if the client needs have been met. They have tested the solution (report) against the criteria. | Candidate has identified qualitative and quantitative evaluation criteria that are appropriate for assessing whether the client needs have been met and testing took full account of the evaluation criteria. |
| Candidate has attempted to evaluate their solution. | Candidate has evaluated their solution and identified some strengths and weaknesses and areas for improvement. | Candidate has evaluated their solution and successfully identified strengths and weaknesses and areas for improvement. |

### Evaluation of the solution – the report

You will have done some of the testing when you were producing the report. Also, some testing should have been carried out when you checked that the information you had obtained from interviews or research was correct. Often, when you interview someone it is easy to mishear or misinterpret what they say. This is why you should always write up any interviews and get the person interviewed to confirm the information is correct or to tell you what is wrong. Exactly the same thing applies to the content of the report.

**reminder**

If you have already done Unit 1, be careful because this is not exactly the same as what you were asked to do for that unit.

**Figure 2.21** It can be easy to misinterpret what people say in interviews

The marks for this fall under AO3 and are:

| 1 mark | 2 marks | 3 marks |
|---|---|---|
| Candidate has produced a report that displays limited evidence of checking for meaningful content. | Candidate has provided an annotated draft report that shows changes to be made to ensure it is accurate and meaningful. | Candidate has produced a final version of the report that has been checked, amended where necessary, and is meaningful in content. |

The factual correctness needs to be checked by someone from the organisation itself and not by you!

When you do your evaluation you must do it logically, referring to the criteria that you have set and the testing that you have done. To do this logically you should do the following:

■ Look at each evaluation criterion in turn.
■ Ask yourself:
  − Has this been met or not?
  − Where is the evidence to show whether or not it has been met?
  − If it hasn't been met, why not?

If you write up your evaluation of the report in this way, taking each criterion in turn and quoting evidence or reasons for success or failure, then you are more likely to produce a good quality evaluation.

This is a straightforward part of the work on which to gain marks. What moderators do not want to see is the student who just states 'I think' or 'as you can see, it meets the evaluation criteria' without showing any real understanding or providing evidence to back up what they are saying.

It is useful in this unit to be able to get comments from the person for whom you have written the report, or if this is not possible then a similar person, i.e. someone who is a senior manager and who is not an ICT specialist.

## Standard ways of working

All Applied specifications require students to adopt what are called 'standard ways of working'. These are, basically, best practice that should be followed when working with ICT. This specification emphasises certain aspects of standard ways of working in each unit.

In this unit you will notice that copyright law is emphasised. You must make sure that you have permission to use everything that you include in your portfolio and particularly in the report. You may be reproducing diagrams that you got from the organisation, or information from a website. It may also be necessary to include acknowledgements in the list of sources used – where you actually name people who have given you information to use. (See page 94 for the marks allocated for this.)

## Evidence of appropriate written communication in the report

These are the marks given for evidence of appropriate written communication in your report:

| 1 mark | 2 marks | 3 marks |
|---|---|---|
| Candidate has used some technical language in writing the report. | Candidate has used appropriate terminology in writing the report. | Candidate has used appropriate terminology in writing the report and explained the terms used. |

It is important, when producing your report, that you consider its readability for the intended level of reader. If you have difficulty with explaining something clearly in the report then use diagrams wherever you can to illustrate what you mean. However, when you do this make sure that the diagrams have titles and are clearly labelled.

Also remember to use a suitable font and to include only screenshots that can be read without the aid of a magnifying glass! Nothing annoys a reader more than having to try to decipher the content of a report because it slows up their reading! One good way to check that the report is readable is to give it to someone who really knows nothing about the subject and see if they can understand it. Anything you need to explain to them, the chances are you need to explain more clearly in the report.

## And finally ...

Remember to check the following:

- All of the elements are present in your portfolio and in a sensible order.
- The research section and the draft and final reports are all clearly labelled.
- You have acknowledged all research sources.
- You have updated and explained any changes to your initial time plan and included all actions that you took. This should include anything that you had to go back and re-do at the end or extra information you had to go and find out.
- There is evidence to support everything that you have done, for example, that you used the software to produce the index, and that you proofread the report yourself.

# 3 Data handling

**The specification for this unit states that you will use relational database management software to:**

► find, select and manipulate data
► use numerical data in large and small data sets
► develop and present information
► communicate information in a way that is suited to the audience
► understand the purpose and uses of databases in organisations
► evaluate the suitability of information for a client.

► We all use databases in our lives. They may not all be computerised databases, and we may not have created them ourselves, but we are all users of information and much of the information that we make use of comes from a database of one type or another. Take the following examples of things that you might do:

■ find the time of a train or bus
■ order a product from an online store
■ search for an article on the Internet
■ look for a name and address of someone or a telephone number
■ find a particular book in a library
■ find the price of tickets for an event and book a seat.

**Figure 3.1** Examples of using databases

All of these activities are about asking/finding out information, and the chances are that the data used to produce the information that you want are being stored in a database.

This unit concentrates on assessing your ability to understand:

- how data can be in different forms
- how to ensure its reliability and integrity
- how it can be formatted and structured in different ways
- how it can be manipulated to produce information
- and, most importantly, how the information can be presented in such a way that it is good information and therefore usable.

## Assessment for this unit

▶ You will have to produce a portfolio of work to provide evidence for assessment. You will be assessed against the four assessment objectives:

- A01 Practical capability in applying ICT (18 marks)
- A02 Knowledge and understanding of ICT systems and their roles in organisations and society (10 marks)
- A03 Application of knowledge, skills and understanding to produce solutions to ICT problems (28 marks)
- A04 Evaluation of ICT solutions and your own performance (14 marks)

The objectives are the same for all of the units that you will study. What changes is the weighting on the different objectives, so, for example, A02 has less weighting in Unit 3 than in Unit 1 and A03 has a higher weighting in this unit than in either Units 1 or 2. Unit 3 demands a far greater need for the application of knowledge and understanding than either of the other units for the single AS award. This is because there is more emphasis on the need to design a solution to meet the needs of a client and the detail that is contained within this design work.

As this is an internally assessed unit, your teacher carries out an assessment of your work. Then the examination board checks the standard of the marks given by your school to make sure that all of the assessment across the different schools and colleges in the country is to the same standard. Notice that the number of marks for your practical skills is only 21 out of the possible 70, so you cannot get away with just being good at using a piece of software. What you show that you understand in your writing is also very important, as is the way that you plan and carry out your work.

# Background knowledge needed

## What is a database?

► As previously mentioned, one thing that you have to be able to understand is just what a database is and what makes it different from data. Data are strings of numbers or facts or records with no particular order. They make no sense in their own right and trying to find an individual value in the data would be extremely difficult. Imagine having the names and telephone numbers of everyone who you know jumbled up and written down completely randomly in a notebook: how long would it take you to find the number that you wanted?

A database is data that have had a structure associated with them. So, if we take the example of names and telephone numbers, if you organise the names and numbers into alphabetical order of surname, in other words give the data a structure, they become a database. From this you can tell that a telephone directory is a database. It is possible to search for an individual name or to find an address. You can also search for the names and numbers of plumbers or electricians, or the local council library services.

Remember what one of the advantages of using ICT is: it reduces the time taken to perform tasks that we can do manually but are very inefficient to do in this way.

### reminder

An ICT system is made up of:
■ hardware
■ software
■ people
■ procedures and
■ data.

### definition

**Data**

Data comprise raw facts and figures, or sets of values, measurements or records of transactions. These values, measurements or records have no meaning and have not been processed. Note that data is plural; the singular of data is datum.

**Figure 3.2** Yell.com

**Figure 3.3** BT online

## definition

**Database**

A database is 'a (large) collection of data items and the links between them, structured in a way that allows it to be accessed by a number of application programs. The term is used loosely to describe any collection of data.'[1]

'an organised body of related information'
http://wordnet.princeton.edu/perl/webwn

'A set of data that is structured and organised for quick access to specific information.'
http://www.umkc.edu/registrar/sis/glossary.asp

'A database is a collection of information stored in a computer in a systematic way, such that a computer program can consult it to answer questions. The software used to manage and query a database is known as a database management system (DBMS).'
http://en.wikipedia.org/wiki/Database

---

[1] The BCS Glossary of ICT and Computing terms (11th edition)

## TASK 1

Working with someone else, with one of you using the local telephone directory and the other using the following web page:
http://www.thephonebook.bt.com/publisha.content/en/find/index.publisha,
which is the web address for BT's online version of the telephone directory, look up the telephone numbers for your local library, doctors' surgery, an electrician, the local branch of Boots the chemist and the local supermarket.

Which is the quicker way of doing things? Why is it quicker?

## Databases in organisations

At one time, the different departments in organisations used to all keep their own data. For example, in one organisation you might have found the following:

- The transport department would keep details of customer names, addresses and delivery instructions to organise the delivery of goods.
- The sales department would keep details of customer names, addresses and phone numbers to be able to send out mailshots and deal with customer orders.
- The accounts department would also need customer details so that they could send out invoices to customers. They would need to keep details of what had been ordered.

The individual departments would organise the data in different ways. The accounts department would probably use invoice numbers, whereas the transport department might use postcode area to structure the data. It is easy to see from the above example that there would be a lot of data that were stored more than once (e.g. customer name and address) and this could cause all sorts of problems. If the customer moved house, which department would find out first? Would they tell the other departments? Could there be the situation where there were three different addresses, all for the same customer? What happens after a customer stops using the company? Does each department remember to delete the old data and do they remember to regularly back up their own data?

Looking at what makes up an ICT system, hardware and software can always be replaced. So can people. Procedures can be introduced or changed, but data cannot be replaced unless the database is backed up regularly. An organisation's data are the most important things that it owns and having reliable data, free from errors and inconsistencies is one of the most important things that any organisation tries to achieve.

### The value of data

The following case studies illustrate how lapses in data security can occur.

## case study 1
▶ Citibank

### Citibank admits: we've lost the backup tape
By Andrew Orlowski
Published Tuesday 7 June 2005 09:06 GMT

The retail finance division of Citigroup has admitted that a backup tape containing personal information on almost 4 million customers in the US has gone missing. The United Parcel Service lost the tape on May 2nd, and it hasn't been seen since. CitiFinancial only noticed the tape was missing on May 20. The tape contains Social Security numbers and transaction histories on both open and closed accounts at the bank's lending branches in the US.

Citigroup says it has no reason to believe the tape has been stolen, but alarmingly, the tape hasn't shown up at any UPS depot despite six weeks of searching.

The company admitted that it doesn't use encryption on its electronic transmissions, nor explained why it took so long to notify the public.

Earlier this year a backup tape belonging to Ameritrade went astray, with personal information on 200,000 customers, Time Warner lost a tape containing information on 600,000 individuals, and Bank of America and Wachovia suffered a data breach affecting 100,000 customers each in May.

## case study 2
► Starbucks

**Figure 3.4** Starbucks

## Starbucks data missing
Company says laptops with employees' records are lost
By Craig Harris
P-I Reporter
Published Saturday, 4 November, 2006

Starbucks Corp., the world's largest coffee retailer, said Friday that laptops containing the names, addresses and Social Security numbers of 60,000 current and former employees are missing.

The company said it has been unable to find four out-of-use laptops at its Seattle headquarters, a nine-floor building in the Sodo area. Two of those computers had personal information on employees hired before Dec. 31, 2003, said Valerie O'Neil, a Starbucks spokeswoman. She did not know what information was on the other two computers. Most of the affected employees worked in the United States; a few worked in Canada.

O'Neil said the company first realised the computers were missing Sept. 6, when an employee 'went to retrieve them in the normal course of business.' She said the laptops were password-protected and still could be in the building.

She said that Starbucks is notifying affected employees, and that the company waited nearly two months to disclose the problem while a thorough internal investigation was completed to try to find the computers.

'There is no indication we have that these laptops are with someone who intends to use the information,' O'Neil said.

Of the 60,000 people affected, 10,000 are still employed by the company.

Pam Dixon, executive director of San Diego-based World Privacy Forum, said Starbucks waited far too long to notify its employees.

'You don't want a problem like this to get out of control,' said Dixon, whose non-profit organisation focuses on research and privacy. 'It's just better to err on the side of caution and to really inform your employees and take care of them … The right thing to do is to focus on the victims. You shouldn't care so much about your brand that you don't think of the victims.'

Abe Kleinfeld, chief executive of San Francisco-based nCircle, said security breaches occur almost daily across the country.

The missing computers at Starbucks follow a string of high-profile losses of sensitive information elsewhere. In May, personal data on about 28.6 million U.S. military veterans were stolen from the residence of a Department of Veterans Affairs analyst who improperly took the information home. The next month, a laptop containing fingerprints and Social Security numbers of Internal Revenue Service employees was lost. Last year, Time Warner Inc. said data on 600,000 current and former employees stored on computer backup tapes were lost, and a thief stole a Boeing Co. computer that had personal information of 161,000 current and former workers.

►

## case study 2
▶ continued

Since February 2005, data breaches involving at least 97 million names have occurred, said Kleinfeld, who runs a network security firm.

Kleinfeld said that while Starbucks made news Friday, the problem soon will happen to someone else.

'It's just a little embarrassing, but none of this is causing enough incentive for companies to do something about it,' Kleinfeld said. 'Laws will need to change to create penalties for this even happening in the first place … It happens every single day and people have become numb to it.'

O'Neil said Starbucks is offering each of the affected employees a free credit protection service through Equifax Inc. O'Neil did not know how much that would cost Starbucks.

Ironically, Equifax said in June that a company laptop containing its employee names and Social Security numbers was stolen.

These case studies show how just losing a backup tape of data or computers themselves can have serious repercussions for an organisation, but what about when you don't have a backup?

## case study 3

A firm of builders had their office broken into one night and their computer was stolen. On the hard disk of the machine was the only copy they had of customer details and of invoice details, including whether or not the invoices had been paid. The builders' firm went bankrupt within six months of the burglary as a result of not being able to send out invoices or contact customers to see whether or not they had paid.

### TASK 2

Search for other stories about data being lost or stolen – you will be surprised at just how many there are!

You can see from these case studies that data are extremely important for organisations, and anything ICT can do to make them more secure or dependable – as well as easier to access – is a benefit.

## Benefits of databases

Computerised databases have been used for many years and they have provided organisations with many benefits. They allow organisations to centralise all of their data in one 'place' and to take control of them. They are used to separate the data from the programs using them, so many programs can all make use of the same pool of data without the need for each program (or, in fact, department) to have its own data. Software that is used to manage and organise data is called Database Management Software (or System) – DBMS for short. There are several different types of DBMS, which are appropriate for different situations, but by far the most commonly used today are RDBMSs.

## What is an RDBMS?

RDBMS stands for Relational Database Management Software (or System) and is software that allows data to be organised by using the relationships that exist between items of data. There are several benefits of using RDBMS rather than other types of database software. These can be seen in Table 3.1.

| |
|---|
| 1. Data are independent from programs |
| 2. Less redundant or duplicated data |
| 3. Greater data consistency |
| 4. Improved quality of management information |
| 5. Single input of data saves time on data input |
| 6. Increased productivity because it is easier to produce reports |
| 7. It allows different access rights to different items of data |

**Table 3.1** Advantages of using an RDBMS

### Task 3

Find out how many different makes of RDBMS you can find for sale at the moment. Can you find out which is most popular with small businesses and individual users, and which with large businesses?

## How RDBMSs are used and their benefits

An RDBMS works on the principle that data are stored in tables. Each table is about a 'thing' (called an entity) about which the organisation wants to store data. Tables are connected together on the basis of relationships between the entities that they represent.

## Examples

**1.** In a sales order system, data will be needed about customers and the orders they make. So, customers and orders are entities.

There can be many occurrences of customer (the organisation has many customers) and a customer can make many orders. There is a relationship between the customer entity and the order entity that is called a one-to-many relationship.

This can be shown in a diagram like that below:

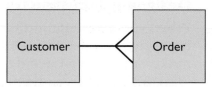

**Figure 3.5** One-to-many entity relationship diagram

**2.** A teacher in a school teaches many different students and one student can be taught by several different teachers. The entities here are student and teacher, and the relationship between them is many-to-many, as shown below:

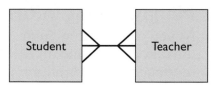

**Figure 3.6** Many-to-many entity relationship diagram

## Many-to-many relationships

Many-to-many relationships cause problems because they do not get rid of duplicated data. However, one of the advantages of a relational database is that it can be set up to avoid duplicating data. Take this example of teachers and students:

| Teacher | Student | Subject | Class |
|---|---|---|---|
| Mrs Jones | Peter Smith | Biology | 1A |
| Miss Farman | Fran Edwards | Chemistry | 2C |
| Mr Hogg | Jeremy Fisher | Physics | 3B |
| Mr Hogg | Jack Dempsey | Physics | 3B |
| Miss Farman | Darren Gough | Chemistry | 2C |
| Mrs Jones | George Francis | Biology | 1A |
| Mr Hogg | Helen Owen | Physics | 3B |
| Miss Farman | Charlene Phillips | Chemistry | 2C |
| Mrs Jones | Sharon Brown | Physics | 1A |

In this example, the teachers' names are duplicated because one teacher can teach many students and one student can have many teachers.

What joins the two entities together is the entity 'class', because one class can have many students and one teacher can teach many classes. So, a diagram to illustrate this would look like that in Figure 3.7:

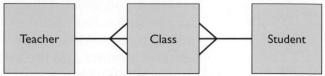

**Figure 3.7** Using an extra entity in a relational database

### Designing data structures

When you are designing your own data structures (the name given to the tables and relationships between them) you must make sure that you avoid having any many-to-many relationships. This is the most likely reason for you to need to use three tables in your data structure. This allows you to break down a many-to-many relationship into two separate one-to-many or many-to-one relationships, like the example shown on the previous page. Doing this results in less redundant data and greater efficiency for solutions because searching and sorting becomes faster.

## Management information and RDBMS

As you can see from Table 3.1 on page 106, there are advantages of using an RDBMS that relate to the quality of management information produced and the ease of report production. Companies acquire large amounts of data over the years and they can gain business advantages if they can make use of this data. Just think about how much data are collected every time you make a purchase in a supermarket and think about the fact that the company collects this data from every customer, using every store, every day. The amount of data stored about buying habits – what, where, when – is vast. Store cards were introduced by many of the large supermarkets as a way of increasing the value of the data that they were collecting, for example in order to gain customer loyalty.

### Data warehousing and data mining

A **data warehouse** is where large amounts of data are stored together. **Data mining** is 'the analysis of a large amount of data in a data warehouse to provide new information. For example, by using loyalty cards that connect purchases to a particular customer, supermarkets can gather information about the buying habits of individual customers. Combining all this information about customers helps them to establish long term trends'.[2] It also allows the company to carry out customised marketing of products that they know you are the 'type' of person to buy!

2 The BCS Glossary of ICT and Computing terms (11th edition)

## Data and Information

Data that are stored about entities are entered into fields in a data table. Data can be of several different types. The AS specification lists the following types of data that you are expected to learn about and be able to use:

- Number
- Currency
- Text (string)
- Date
- Boolean (true/false)

Some examples of what is meant by each data type are shown in the following box:

---

## Data types

### Number

1, 2, 26, 234567, 123.45, 1076.34567, –234, –21.876, 0

Numbers can be positive or negative. They can be whole numbers or decimals and they can have any number of decimal places. The format you use for numbers depends on the purpose for which they are used.

### Currency

This simply indicates that the numbers that are stored are of a special type. The value may be prefixed by a unit, for example:

£2,425.26, €4,527.33, 3712.44

### Text

This is used for any form of word(s) or an alphanumeric string (where the data contain both letters and numbers). For example:

Name, address, stock code (ABC123)

### Date

This includes the day, month and year, and also hours and minutes. Again, the format the data is used in depends on what it is required for.

### Boolean

The true or false type of data. This is used, for example, when you want to store data about whether or not an invoice has been paid, whether or not an order has been dispatched, whether or not a credit card number has been included, or whether or not a receipt is required. This data type cannot be formatted in any way and how it is displayed is part of the DBMS. In the Microsoft® Access™ RDBMS this is the Yes/No data type.

---

The following screenshot shows the data types available when using Access™:

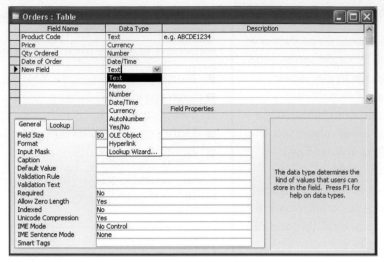

**Figure 3.8** Data types available in Microsoft® Access™

## Data formats

As seen above, each data type can be stored in several different formats. What formats are available for you to use will partly depend on the RDBMS you are using, but the most common ones are listed in the specification, as follows:

| Data type | Examples of data formats |
|---|---|
| Text | fixed or limited length, unlimited length or memo |
| Number | integer, long |
| Date | dd/mm/yy, dd/mm, day month year |
| Currency | £ (pounds), £ and p (pounds and pence), $ (dollars), or e (euros). |

The following screenshots show some of the data types and formats available if using the Microsoft® Access™ RDBMS.

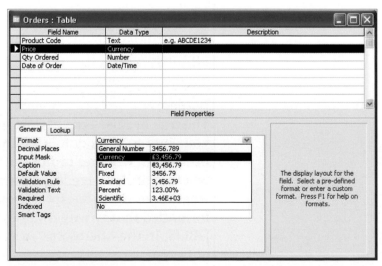

**Figure 3.9** Currency formats

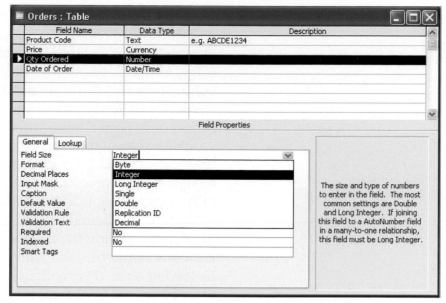

**Figure 3.10** Number formats

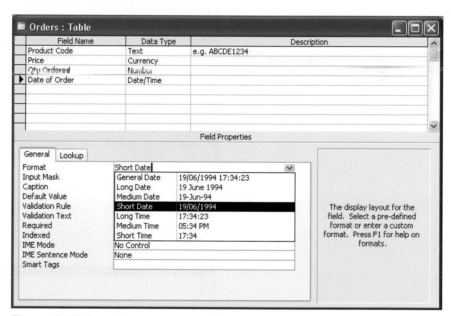

**Figure 3.11** Date formats

You need to understand about data types and formats so that when you are producing the solution for your client, you will be able to select the most appropriate data types and formats that will best suit their needs. You will have to explain why you have used the data types that you have, and why you have chosen to format the data in the way that you have done. It will be very important for you to find out what the data that are used by your client are like and whether the formats used at present are correct or whether they need any changes making. Collecting sample documents (including data) currently used by your client is a good way of looking at the data types and formats needed.

## Ensuring only correct and valid data are entered

As mentioned previously, it is very important that an organisation or an individual can rely on the data, which are stored and used to produce information, being correct and valid. These two words **do not** mean the same thing!

Validity of data is about the data being within expected ranges or expected types. There are many different types of validation check that can be used, e.g. range, type, presence, and format checks. For example, on an online entry form for a competition, people have to enter their age. The competition is only open to people in the 15 to 30 year age group. A sensible validation rule would be that the age must be greater or equal to 15 and less than 31. If someone tried to enter the age of 23 then this would be valid data, but if they entered 35 it would be invalid data. (For more information on data validation, see *Information and Communication Technology for AQA AS Level* (Second Edition), Hodder Murray, 2006, pages 136–9.)

An RDBMS allows you to build in validation rules when you are specifying the data types and formats for each field in a table. In other words, validation can be carried out by the software because it is simply checking data against certain rules.

The following screenshots show validation rules that have been set up for a range of data types:

### TASK 4

What is meant by a **default** value?

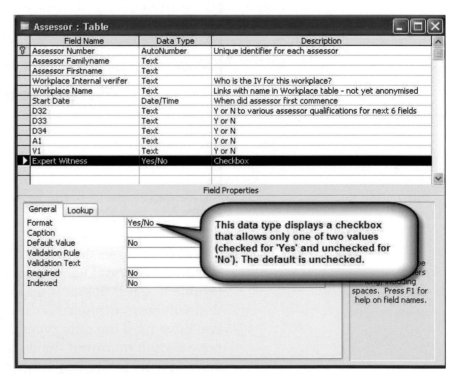

**Figure 3.12** Validation rule for text entry

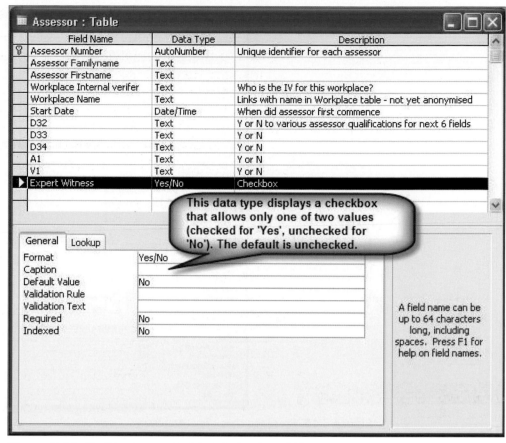

**Figure 3.13** Yes/No data type with default value of No

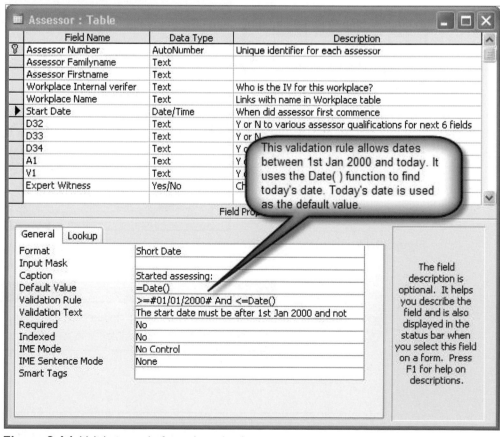

**Figure 3.14** Validation rule for a date check

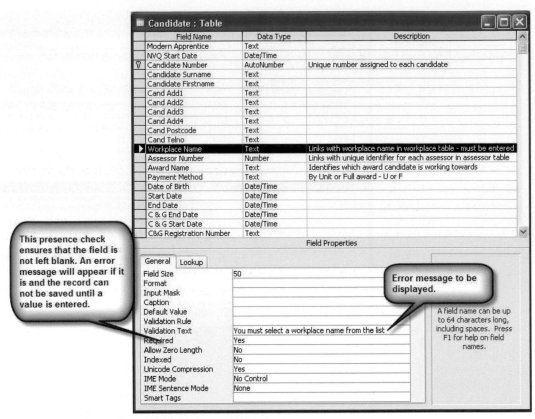

This presence check ensures that the field is not left blank. An error message will appear if it is and the record can not be saved until a value is entered.

Error message to be displayed.

**Figure 3.15** Presence check for data entry

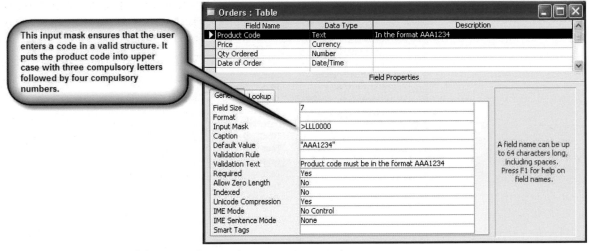

This input mask ensures that the user enters a code in a valid structure. It puts the product code into upper case with three compulsory letters followed by four compulsory numbers.

**Figure 3.16** Input mask for a product code

## TASK 5

**Item 37** on the CD-ROM is an exercise for you to see if you can decide what type of check would be suitable for different items of data.

Designing test data to test whether a validation rule works and only allows valid data to be entered into a database requires careful planning. The following are some data that could be used to test the example of the age field in the outline entry form for a competition discussed above:

- 24 – a valid number
- 14, 15, 16, 29, 30 and 31 – to test the extremes and the construction of the validation rule
- 78, 999 and −17 – invalid data
- xx – invalid alphabetical data

N.B. Invalid data are sometimes called erroneous data. When you carry out your testing, you will probably not have enough time to be able to show every single test for every field, so you will need to show in your test plan that you do understand how exhaustive testing should be. Marks are lost by people who only test with 'normal/acceptable' data. This is because the purpose of testing is to try to provoke failure so that any errors can be corrected before a solution is given to a client.

## Correctness of data

Correctness is about ensuring that the data that are entered are the data that should have been entered. The term used for checking that data are correct is 'verification'. In other words, the data being entered are verified to make sure that they are exactly what should be entered. Verification has to be carried out by the person actually entering the data into the database, but the software can be used to try to prompt or force people to verify what they have entered. A simple example is when entering a password – you will be asked to enter the password a second time. The two entries will then be checked against each other and only if they are the same will you be allowed to proceed. Two examples of this are given in Figures 3.17 and 3.18:

**Figure 3.17** Setting up a password for an Internet account

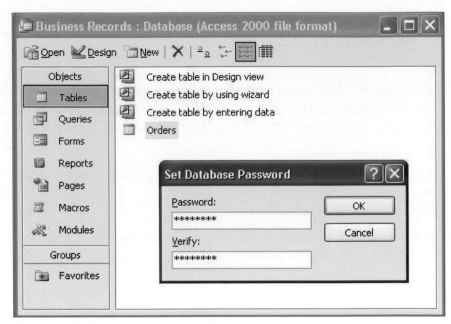

**Figure 3.18** Setting up a password for a database

## reminder

Verification is also frequently used when the piece or item of data being entered is a command to the software. An example of this is when you are asked, 'Are you sure you want to delete 1 record(s)?' It is important to remember that things like mouse clicks and movements are data in the form of instructions, like 'select this item from the list', as you click on a drop-down list.

Figures 3.19 to 3.21 show some examples of verification messages that can be displayed:

## TASK 6

Are the messages provided in the examples in Figures 3.19 – 3.21 appropriate for any type of user? Why?

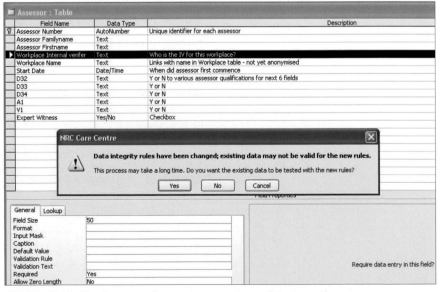

**Figure 3.19** Verification after creating a new validation rule

**Figure 3.20** Verification of cascade delete action

**Figure 3.21** Verification on make table query

## Inputting data

As well as considering the validity and accuracy of the data being entered, you must consider who is going to be entering the data. Data entry must be very carefully considered, not in relation to setting up the system to begin with, but from the point of view of the person who is going to use the database solution you create. Everything that you design relates to the needs of the client and you need to be able to justify your designs on this basis – see A03 in the marking grid on page 139.

Remember that the formats you choose for different items of data will also determine how easy it is for the user to enter the data.

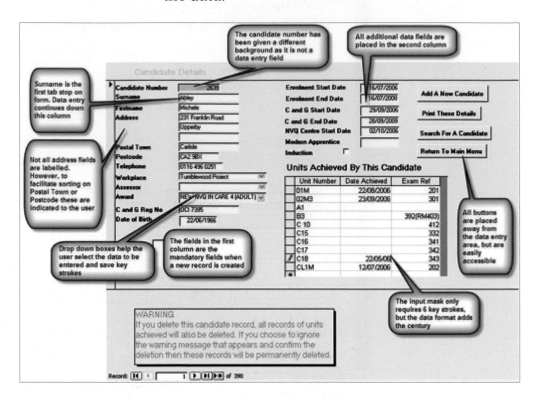

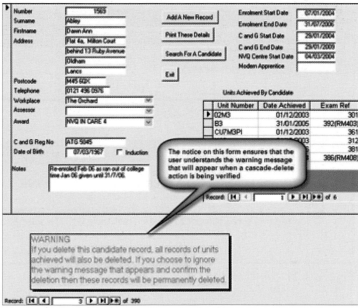

**Figure 3.22** Examples of data input screens

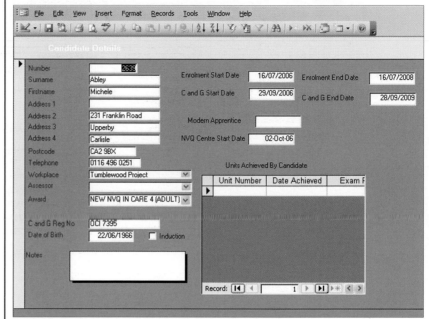

## TASK 5

**Item 10** on the CD-ROM has rules for interface design. Have a look at these rules and then answer the following questions.

Here is a screenshot of an input form designed using the Microsoft® Access™ RDBMS.

1   What are its good points?
2   What are its faults?
3   How easy would it be to use and could you improve it in any way?

**Figure 3.23** An input form designed using RDBMS

## TASK 7

Why does the frequency of use of a solution affect the way in which the interface should be designed?

## So what does make a good interface?

The following points should be considered once you know the characteristics of the user (for example, their dexterity, experience of software packages, eyesight and their predicted frequency of use of the solution):

- Order of data entry – should be logical so the fields are in the same order that they are on, for example, a source document, or in the same order that questions are asked if an order is taken over the telephone.
- Do the fields go across a row and then down, as in reading a book, or down one side of the screen and then down the other?
- Size and type of font used.
- Background colour used.
- Colour and size of areas where data need entering.
- Cursor movement – by mouse click, return key or tab key?
- Size, order and positioning of command buttons and what command words are used – are all commands used in Microsoft® products understandable?
- Constant features on an input screen, e.g. company logo, name of solution, operation, quit or return to main menu.

- How much information is there on one screen? Or, on multiple screens for entry, does data split logically? What do you need to know to be able to decide this?
- Screen size of user as opposed to developer of the solution.

There are all sorts of things to consider and you should be able to show in your annotated design work what you have done and why.

The following screenshots show examples of annotation that explain the features used in the software solution:

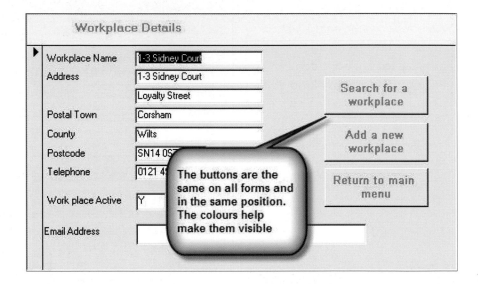

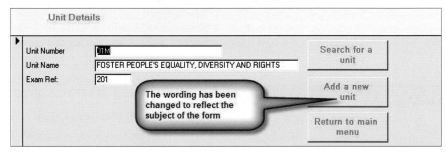

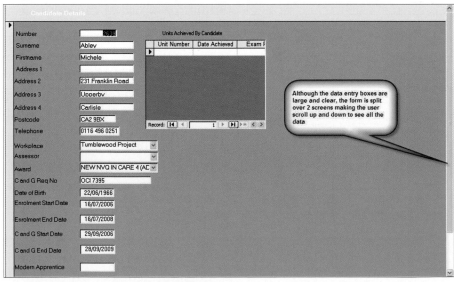

**Figure 3.24** Examples of annotations

## TASK 8

Item **39** on the CD-ROM is an exercise which gives you a set of data to design an entry form for a particular task. This will help you to think about some of the things given above so that you can practise designing your own input screens!

## reminder

The **client** will be the person who asks for the solution; the **user** is the person who actually uses it. So, a dentist may commission a solution but the user may actually be his receptionist.

## TASK 9

A bookshop offers a service to customers to search a database of the books that they stock in their chain of stores around the country so that if a book is not in stock in one branch, then the customer can order it from stock held by another. The customers need to be able to search by author surname, author initials, book title, ISBN number, price, hardback or softback version, publisher and genre or type of book.

Suggest a suitable design for the database to allow a search on any one, or combination of, the above characteristics. Also, think about what data types and formats would be needed.

## Quality of information

As mentioned earlier, if the data are not correct and valid, then the information produced by processing that data will not be of any use. There are also other factors that affect whether the information produced by an ICT system is good or not. One of these is whether the processing of the data has been designed correctly.

In solutions produced using an RDBMS much of the processing carried out will be searching and sorting data to generate lists or produce information about an item.

### Example

A stock database system used online by an electrical retailer is likely to be used to produce information for customers. A customer wants to find the best value 15" flat-screen television that the supplier has in stock. He enters the details that he wants 'all 15" flat-screen televisions costing between £200 and £500 in ascending order of price'. This will require the database to be searched for these items and then sorted by price to provide the information that the customer requires. An RDBMS has the facility to easily produce queries and generate reports, which can be displayed on screen or printed out. This query is what is called a 'parameter query' because there are several parameters that are entered. The parameters here are the fact that it is a television, the price range and the size of the television screen.

If you were designing the data for this solution you would have to make sure that each of the parameters above was stored as a separate item of data or field, otherwise it would not be possible to search using that data as a parameter.

There are different types of queries that can be used, but all of them involve asking questions of the database, basically saying, 'Can you find me x?'. This is what is meant by the title of this unit, 'Data handling' – handling data in such a way as to obtain information from it.

Figures 3.25 to 3.29 show several different types of query that can be used to handle data.

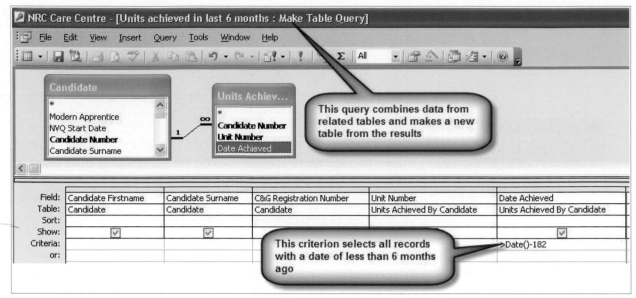

**Figure 3.25**

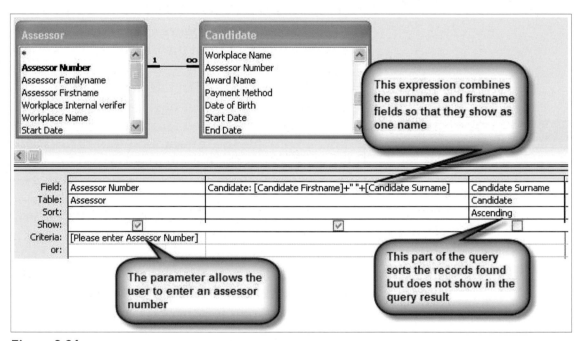

**Figure 3.26**

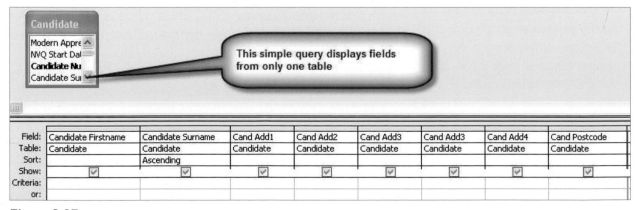

**Figure 3.27**

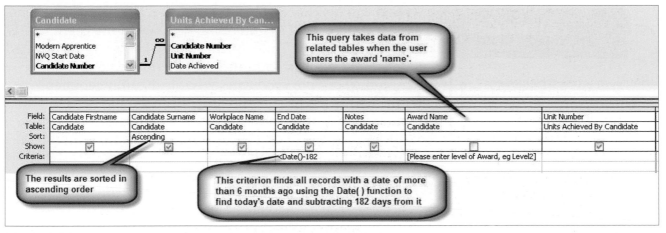

**Figure 3.28**

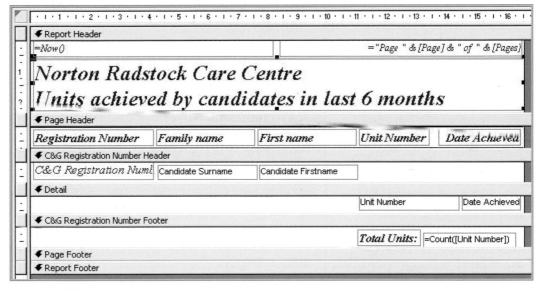

**Figure 3.29**

So handling or processing data is about searching and sorting, and doing calculations in order to provide information, for example:

- totalling the value of items in an order
- working out an average mark
- adding VAT to an invoice.

What processing is required depends on what the client wants in the way of information from the solution.

## Output

The format of the output information also depends on what the client wants. In the example of the bookshop, the customer will probably want to see only the result of the search on the screen, or they may want a printout of the results if there is a list of books resulting from the search. The bookshop may want to save the result of the search to put in an order to another branch or email a request to them.

## TASK 10

**Item 40** on the CD-ROM is an example of an author's summary report sent by their publisher. Work out what data and processing would be required in order to produce it.

When you are doing your investigation into what the client needs, it is important to find out exactly what the client wants as output. Very often students think they know what is wanted or use standard report formats and end up losing marks because they are not producing what is actually required. Designs for reports are often badly put together – see later on in this section for examples of this! Remember too, as in the bookshop example above, there is frequently more than one output required from a solution.

## Reports

The word 'report' is generally used to describe any form of output from an RDBMS. It does not have to be an actual report like the one you have to produce for Unit 2 – it could be an invoice, an order, an appointment, a certificate, a class list, a score sheet, a timetable, or an appointment list. All of these reports can be generated by processing the data correctly and formatting the output into the desired document. Attention to detail is important – remembering to think about putting dates on reports, or the name of the person who produced it, and making sure that the information fits on a page and prints correctly given the printer's characteristics. Reports can be in colour or black and white. They can be printed landscape or portrait and can have logos included or be printed onto headed paper. Reports can also be faxed, emailed, or put onto an Internet site to be printed off as required.

The following screenshots show two reports as a user would see them on screen and as a developer would work on them in what is called 'design view'. Annotation shows particular features used:

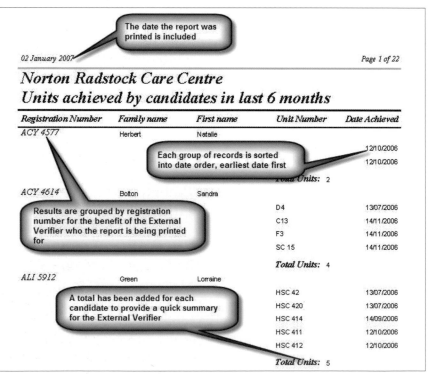

**Figure 3.30** Report as a user would see it

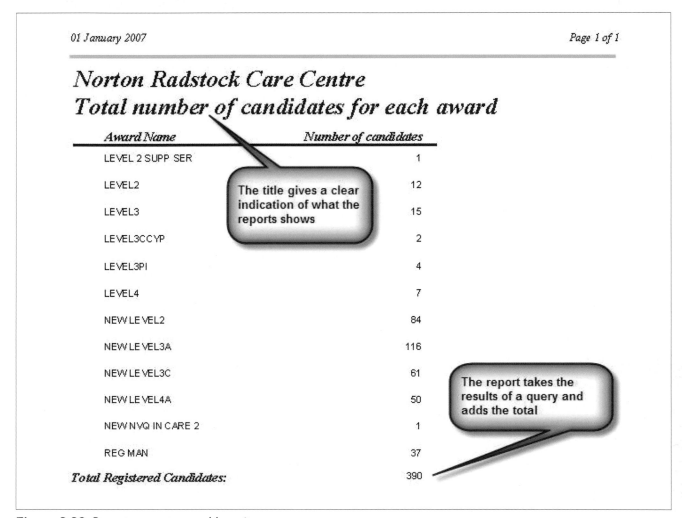

**Figure 3.31** Design view of the report shown in Figure 3.30

01 January 2007                                                          Page 1 of 1

## Norton Radstock Care Centre
## Total number of candidates for each award

| Award Name | Number of candidates |
|---|---|
| LEVEL 2 SUPP SER | 1 |
| LEVEL2 | 12 |
| LEVEL3 | 15 |
| LEVEL3CCYP | 2 |
| LEVEL3PI | 4 |
| LEVEL4 | 7 |
| NEW LEVEL2 | 84 |
| NEW LEVEL3A | 116 |
| NEW LEVEL3C | 61 |
| NEW LEVEL4A | 50 |
| NEW NVQ IN CARE 2 | 1 |
| REG MAN | 37 |
| **Total Registered Candidates:** | 390 |

The title gives a clear indication of what the reports shows

The report takes the results of a query and adds the total

**Figure 3.32** Report as a user would see it

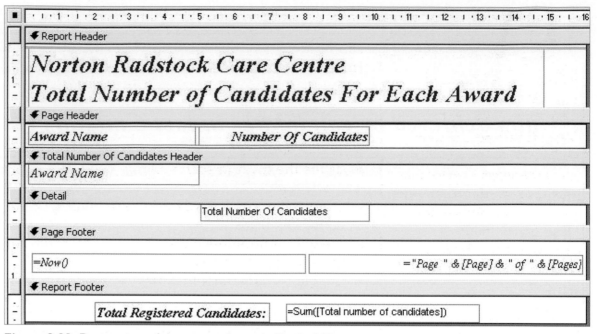

**Figure 3.33** Design view of the report shown in Figure 3.32

## TASK 11

See how many different types of output report you can identify that you think have been generated as a result of a query on an RDBMS, or that you think might or could be generated in this way. One example could be progress reports that you get, or letters to take home about events.

# Skills required

## Software

▶ Obviously, it is important that you are familiar with how to use the RDBMS that will be available to you in your school or college for the work on this unit. There is no requirement for you to use any particular RDBMS. It just has to be relational database software that allows you to produce a solution using multiple tables and relationships.

It may be that you already have quite a high skill level in using the software, but you will have to know and understand:

- what data types and formats are available and how to use them
- how to create data structures, tables and relationships
- how to input, validate and verify data
- how to process data – searching, sorting and performing calculations using queries
- what output formats are available and how to create reports and forms.

There are plenty of textbooks available on how to use the software, such as *Database Projects in Access for Advanced Level 2nd Edition*, by Mott and Rendell, published by Hodder Murray.

The specification states that you must learn to carry out the following activities:

- construct tables
- create data entry forms
- define the fields in each table
- create queries
- produce printed reports and screen output
- define key fields
- use and manipulate data
- use wizards effectively
- use built-in database facilities appropriately.

You will need to be able to use word processing software to write up your portfolio and you will also need to be able to take screenshots, so knowing how to use any specialist software to enable this will be useful. One piece of freeware software is Screenshot Pilot, which can be downloaded from: http://www.colorpilot.com/screenshot.html.

## Researching

In this unit, the research work that you need to carry out centres around two areas:

- making sure that you understand what is meant by data handling and how RDBMSs are used
- discovering what your client wants.

If you have read the first part of this section and done the tasks suggested then you should have covered the first area, so now you need to concentrate on the second.

## TASK 12

To check you do understand, make sure you know what is meant by the following:

1 A database
2 An entity and its attributes
3 A table and fields
4 A relationship
5 Reports
6 Verification and validation
7 Queries
8 User interface design and usability issues
9 Data handling

## Choosing a client and discovering what the client wants

It is vital that you have a real client for this unit and, in fact, for any unit where you are being asked to design a solution for a client. Students who try to make up a client or who act as the client themselves, rarely produce good quality work. The reason for this is that they think they know what is wanted and don't have to go and ask someone, with the result being that they cannot justify the design decisions that they take and so lose marks on A03 – the highest weighted assessment objective for this unit. It also results in lower marks on A04. Students find it difficult to achieve high grades on this unit if they do not get good marks on A03.

You can use the same client that you use for this unit for other units. There are lots of possibilities for clients because so many people make use of databases and this unit does not require you to create anything too complex. Your teacher should be able to help you with finding a client but see if you can find one from one of the following sources:

- friends or family
- part-time job
- organisations you belong to
- charities or voluntary groups
- other teachers or support staff at your school or college.

You shouldn't think that doing things for friends and family is the easy option. It never is because they are always saying things like, 'we'll speak about it later' or, 'you know what I mean'!

It may be possible to have a client that you do not actually have any 'face-to-face' contact with, because today it is so easy to communicate electronically via email, webcams and Skype©, etc.

You do not need or have to produce a full-scale RDBMS with lots of tables and complex queries. This unit is about data handling and two, or more likely, three tables would suffice (although you may have more because they are lookup tables with 1:1 relationships). It is what you do with the data that is important – the validation and verification, processing and output. Doing something relatively simple and self-contained in great detail, with fully customised formats, error messages, reports and forms, is more important than something large that you skim the surface of using only standard forms, reports, etc.

### Research techniques

There are several ways in which you can research what is required by your client:

- by personal interview
- by telephone
- by letter
- by email
- questionnaires
- observation
- paper-based research
- collecting sample documents.

More information on all of these techniques can be found in Chapter 4 of *ICT Coursework for AS Level*, by Barbara Wilson, published by Hodder Murray.

One thing that you may also find that you need is screenshots or printouts from the current system that is being used by your client. It may be that for this unit you are going to be looking at using a subset of an existing database to produce new information that is required from the data already present. It could be that the current system is not well designed and that you are asked to replace a part of it. What you produce does not need to be an entirely new system. You must, however, be able to consider data types and formats, and validation and verification of data input or you will not be able to access all of the available marks.

## Documentation

As with any portfolio that you produce, the aim of the portfolio is to prove to an assessor what you can do, and what you know and understand. It is important that you organise your work well, and that it is all clear and easy to read. There is more help on this in Section 4 of this book – Portfolios (see page 168).

One element of your work, which is worth mentioning at this stage, is screenshots. These must be clear and easy to read, and should not be cropped so that too little is shown of what you have done. Screenshots should also be annotated to describe to the reader what they are providing evidence of. If you can't think of what to write then the chances are that you don't need the screenshot!

Figures 3.34 and 3.35 show examples of screenshots that are unreadable or badly cropped. Figure 3.36 shows a screenshot that is both clear and well cropped.

Using suitable names for tables, queries, forms and reports is extremely important. Deciding on these should be part of your planning.

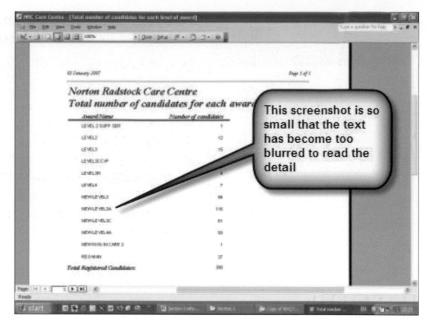

This screenshot is so small that the text has become too blurred to read the detail

**Figure 3.34** An unreadable screenshot

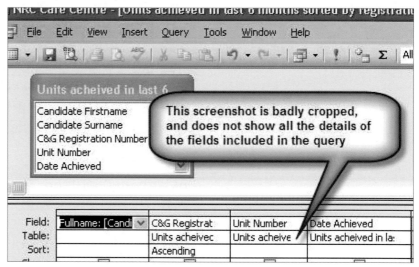

This screenshot is badly cropped, and does not show all the details of the fields included in the query

**Figure 3.35** A badly cropped screenshot

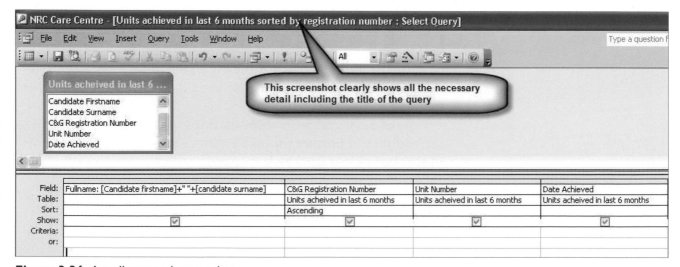

This screenshot clearly shows all the necessary detail including the title of the query

**Figure 3.36** A well cropped screenshot

In particular, for a data handling solution you will need to be able to produce annotated documentation that could include:

- a copy of the agreed data types and formats
- data structures
- inputs
- processing required
- outputs (whether on-screen or hard copy)
- printouts of validation and verification procedures
- printouts of all calculations, formulae and facilities used (annotated to show how/why they have been used)
- printouts of test results, cross-referenced to a test plan
- printouts of the results of processing.

## Design work

Design work for a data handling solution involves designing every item that is necessary for the creation of the solution and also a test plan for testing that the solution does what it is supposed to do in the way that it is supposed to do it.

Design work should always be clear enough for someone else, with a similar level of knowledge of the software that is used, to be able to pick up your designs and create a solution that is exactly what you intended. This is so important in commercial environments because many times people move jobs or are off work sick when they are part-way through a solution, or people do only the design work before the implementation is passed on to another person. Often, solutions need amending some time later and the designs are used to do this. Much time is lost in industry where good design work does not exist and this is a cause of concern for many ICT managers. So get into good habits now and you will find they will stay with you.

Another reason for producing good, clear designs for this type of solution is that database solutions can be very complex and if the data structures and formats are not correct to begin with then it is impossible to produce the information required from them. A simple example of this would be if a manager needed a search to be done by customer postcode and the data table design had only one field for the address, which contained the whole address, including the postcode (as in Figure 3.38). Searching by postcode would not be impossible, but it would be much more complex than necessary and the processing would take a lot longer to do.

The data table in Figure 3.37 has separate address fields for each line of the address, with the postcode in AddressLine4. Searching for a particular postcode in this data table would be much quicker.

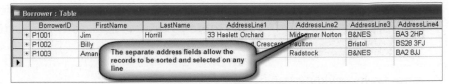

**Figure 3.37** Data table with separate fields for each address line

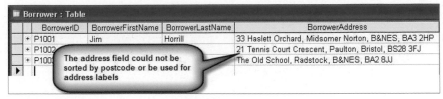

**Figure 3.38** Data table with only one address field

The final reason for completing good designs is that when you are producing a data handling solution there are a lot of individual items that need to be created and often they need to be created in a particular order. For example, tables and relationships need creating before queries, queries before reports. It is usual to produce a solution in logical stages. A suggested order that you might like to follow is shown in the table below:

| Order | Reason |
|---|---|
| Create table setting data formats and key fields | Basis of database |
| Create relationships between tables | To allow for linked fields to be filled simultaneously when data entered |
| Set validation and verification rules for data entry to tables | Means data can be tested when the tables are populated with data |
| Create/customise error messages | So you will know what you have done wrong when you populate the tables and ensures all data used are valid and correct |
| Create data entry forms | Makes entering data into tables easier, allows testing and gives opportunity for improvement |
| Populate tables | Data required to set up solution and allow queries, etc. to be tested |
| Create queries | The processing needed |
| Create further forms linked to input to queries or output from queries | Parameter queries may be linked to forms for input and the same or a different form for output |
| Create report formats | Cannot do this unless input and processing have already been done |

So, when you put together your designs, try to do them in a logical order and present them in this order in your portfolio. Then make yourself a checklist of everything that you need to create in the order that you need to create it. This will help you to stick to a time plan and get everything done on schedule.

## Testing

Testing also needs to be designed. A test plan should be created that includes as a minimum the following information:

- test number
- purpose of test
- data to be used
- expected outcome
- actual outcome.

Remember that the purpose of testing is always to try to provoke failure of a solution, so test data must include valid and invalid data and actions. Always think about why you are doing a particular test, its purpose, and what you expect to happen when particular data are used.

Good testing is based on testing against the evaluation criteria that you have set which are based on ensuring that the client's requirements are met. (This is covered in greater depth in Chapters 11 and 12 of *ICT Coursework for AS Level*, by Wilson.)

The specification states that your testing should check that:

- acceptable data input values (including maximum and minimum values) can be entered
- unacceptable data values are automatically rejected
- all facilities provided by the solution are functional
- all facilities/formulae produce the correct results
- the solution meets the needs of the client.

Always remember that if your solution is meant to be able to generate an invoice or other form of report, then there is evidence that it does actually do this. It is surprising how many students forget to do this. They get bogged down in too many validation/verification/button depression tests and forget what the solution is supposed to do. Do not expect to get good marks if you make this mistake!

**Item 41** on the CD-ROM provides a testing template that you may find helpful.

## Evaluation

If this is the first unit that you are studying, then you need to understand that evaluation has two parts to it: evaluating your own performance and evaluating the solution itself.

There is more information in the assessment part of this section, but remember that evaluation is straightforward if you have good evaluation criteria and testing, and a clear idea of the client's requirements for the solution. In other words, when you get to the point of carrying out your evaluation of the solution, if you haven't put the time and effort into the other items then it is unlikely that your evaluations will gain many marks either!

## Standard ways of working

In this unit, standard ways of working are concerned particularly with keeping data secure and private, and with the sensible naming of items within the database solution.

The reason why data security and privacy are particularly important is that databases are often used to store personal information. Controlling who has access to what data is always important when personal data are stored. Even if the data are not personal they may be commercially sensitive and access may again need to be controlled. To ensure data integrity, who is allowed to amend, update or delete data within a database is critical. All of these aspects should be considered as appropriate to the solution that you are creating.

---

### TASK 13

1. What does 'levels of access' mean? What are different levels of access?
2. Find out how you can create different levels of access to data using the software that you will be using to create your solution.
3. The design of a database solution can help to make controlling access to data easier or harder to enable. Can you think how these different levels of security could be achieved at the design stage?

---

The other issue that you should consider is the names that you use for different items in your database solution. For instance, think about the naming of tables, queries, forms and reports. These names should indicate to a third person what the purpose of the object is. For example, whether it is:

- a query or a table
- about customers or products
- concerned with adding or deleting data.

---

### TASK 14

Have a look at some database solutions that either you have created or someone else has created.

1. Are the names used sensible?
2. If not, why not?
3. Devise your own naming convention to use for your own solution.

---

# Assessment

▶ This part of the book takes you through just what you need to produce as evidence in your portfolio and explains what marks are awarded for. Where possible, it follows the order in which you need to complete the work, the exception being the guidance on time management and planning.

## What you have to produce

For this unit you have to produce a portfolio of evidence that contains the following elements:

- A plan for the work to be completed, showing what needs to be carried out, the sequence of activities and an estimate of the time involved.
- A record to show whether this time plan has been followed and any adjustments made in order to complete the tasks.
- A description of the chosen client and the task(s) which they require undertaking, including why the task is suitable to be solved using relational database management software.
- The input, output and processing requirements for the solution.
- The evaluation criteria for the solution to enable judgement of how well the solution will meet the client needs.
- A test plan to check that the solution meets the evaluation criteria and, therefore, the client needs. The test plan must show what is to be tested and why, the expected results and the data to be used.
- A description of the software to be used, including why it is suitable for solving the tasks for the client.
- Evidence of, and justification for, the data structures, types and formats used in the solution.
- Evidence of the:
  - input methods used, i.e. forms, including how the correctness and validity of data is ensured
  - processing, i.e. queries used, calculations made
  - outputs, i.e. forms and reports
  - features, including error messages, that improve the usability of the solution and its suitability for the client, and explanations of how these meet the client needs.
- Evidence of the results gained by testing the solution, and any steps taken to correct errors and/or make other changes to ensure that the solution meets the client needs.
- Evaluation of the solution produced, using evidence from testing the solution, to show whether the client needs and the evaluation criteria have, or have not, been met.
- An evaluation of your own performance when completing the portfolio and following your plan.
- Evidence of having used standard ways of working. In particular, how security and backup issues have been

## reminder

Item 38 on the CD-ROM provides a list of what you have to produce in your portfolio.

## reminder

If you look at the examination board website http://www.aqa.org.uk you will probably find the date that the board expects the marks for portfolio work to be in. It is no use thinking that all of the time up to then is available to you because the marks have to **arrive** by that date and your teacher will have all of their marking and administration to do before submission to the exam board. So listen to the date that the teacher gives you!

addressed and how you have organised and managed your own work effectively.

■ Evidence of appropriate written communication throughout the portfolio.

This bulleted list is very similar to the list of contents for any of the portfolio units which require the production of a solution for a client. The only differences stem from the content that refers directly to this being a solution created using relational database management software.

Your portfolio will be assessed against the four assessment objectives listed earlier on page 100.

■ A01 is what your practical ability in using the software is assessed against, so you will need to prove that you have actually built the solution.

■ A02 is looking at how well you have researched the client needs, and the inputs, processes and outputs needed to meet the client's requirements.

■ A03 is concerned with your ability to design a solution that meets the client needs, and is where there are most marks available – 28 out of the total 70 marks.

■ A04, as in other units, is concerned with planning, time management, testing, evaluation and written communication.

## Planning

When you are planning your work, make sure that you have a clear understanding of what you have to do in the available time. You need to make sure that you leave sufficient time for things to not go quite as well as you imagine they will. Leaving a little spare time at the end of the period of time that your teacher has given you to complete the work would be sensible, just in case you have any problems. A typical thing to happen is that you don't leave enough time for testing and correcting errors, and then you have difficulty in finding time to complete the evaluation. If this happens you lose marks.

The record should show where you got behind, or in front of, your time plan, and how you adjusted the plan to take account of delays or how you spent the extra time you had available.

Be honest! The exam board is looking to see whether you have learnt from what you have done. For example, many students often underestimate how long it takes to find the information that they need for describing the inputs, processes and outputs required or for getting detailed knowledge of the data formats and validation rules needed.

Unlike Unit 1, there is no split into investigation time and controlled conditions, so it is even more important that you plan your time carefully yourself. It may be that your teacher gives you some interim deadlines to help you, or it may be left entirely up to you, in which case you must definitely try not to leave things to the last minute. Work at this standard cannot be rushed over a weekend or be done the night before you have to submit it. There is just too much to do, and you need to give yourself the chance to look back at work already completed and improve it. The box below contains a quote from the Principal Moderator's report from June 2006:

… candidates need to produce some kind of time plan, showing how they intend to use their time in order to produce their portfolio of evidence. This may be combined with the evidence which describes the actions that they need to take to produce the portfolio of evidence (referred to as 'the problem'). To gain the higher marks the candidate should include not only an estimated time of completion for each action planned, but should update this at frequent intervals to show that they are monitoring their progress and making any necessary adjustments. They will gain maximum marks if they can explain why any deadlines have been missed and what action has been taken to get back on track for the final deadline. Perfect time planning is not expected of candidates at this stage of their learning and it is far better for candidates to be honest than to pretend that everything has gone to schedule.

AQA Chair of Examiners Report Applied ICT June 2006

As mentioned in the bulleted list on page 135, you need to include:

- A plan for the work to be done, showing what needs to be carried out, the sequence of activities and an estimate of the time involved.
- A record to show whether this time plan has been followed and any adjustments made in order to complete the tasks.

This table is a section taken from the marking grid that your teacher will almost certainly use to assess your work:

| I mark | 2 marks | 3 marks |
|---|---|---|
| Candidate has provided a brief description of actions taken to solve the problem. | Candidate has described actions taken to solve the problem. | Candidate has clearly described actions taken to solve the problem and shown a clear understanding of what they have done and why. |
| Candidate has provided limited evidence of time management or planning. | Candidate has provided some evidence of time management and planning. They have met some deadlines and have shown that they understand the need to monitor their progress. | Candidate has provided strong evidence of time management and planning, fully monitored their progress and met deadlines. Reasons for any missed deadlines have been explained. |

If you have already completed Unit 1 or Unit 2 and been examined on either of them, how did you get on? Was time management and planning a weak area that you could improve on?

If you look at the marking grid given on the previous page you will see that there are three marks for describing the actions that you took to 'solve the problem' and three marks for the time planning. In this case your 'problem' is producing the portfolio and so you need to describe what you did in order to complete the work, as well as when and why.

The following is a list of some of the things you might need to start with doing in order to produce your portfolio:

- Read up in the textbook about what you need to do for this unit and make a time plan.
- Learn about how to use the software you need for completing a solution and what it is possible to do using it – use a suitable 'hands on' guide.
- Make sure you understand what is meant by 'data handling' and how complex or big the solution has to be.
- Think of ideas for who to approach for a possible data handling task.
- Organise to visit Mrs Molyneux to interview her about the task she wants doing and observe her at work.
- Go and visit Mrs Molyneux.
- Write up interview notes and send to her for confirmation.

This is just the start of all the things you need to do – there are other things that you could be doing at the same time. For example, looking at sample database solutions, the input forms used, the processing needed and the reports created.

This is really the only time Gantt charts are useful in portfolios – when you want to show how several different activities will overlap in terms of the time that is needed for them. (**Item 34** on the CD-ROM provides Gantt Project software that you can use.)

If you look back at the example of part of a time plan given in Section 1 (see page 36) this will give you ideas for producing your own schedule.

## The background and the task

The list of items that you have to provide evidence for includes:

- A description of the chosen client and the task(s) which they require undertaking, including why the task is suitable to be solved using relational database management software.
- A description of the software that you will use, including why it is suitable for solving the tasks for the client.

You will find this easy to do if you have done your research carefully and you have obtained a real client. If you try to make up a situation and a client, it is always easy to tell that you have done this by what you write and the way that you write it. Never do this! Tell your teacher if you are stuck and they can always help you by being your client themselves or by getting another member of staff to act as one. Don't be tempted to just get a friend to do it.

The assessment objective covered by these points is AO2, which counts for a maximum of 10 marks on Unit 3. The marking grid that your teacher will probably use is shown in this table:

| 1 mark | 2 marks | 3 marks | 4 marks |
|---|---|---|---|
| Candidate has partially described the organisation/background but important details are missing. The candidate does not show any real appreciation of who the client is. | Candidate has described the organisation/background sufficiently to show some understanding of the client. | Candidate has fully described the organisation/background and shows full understanding of the client. | |
| Candidate has provided a list of the tasks for which the solution is to be developed. | Candidate has provided a simple description of the tasks for which the solution is to be developed, showing some understanding of what the solution is to produce. | Candidate has provided a detailed description of the tasks for which the solution is to be developed. It is clear that the candidate fully understands what the solution is required to produce. | From the detailed description it is clear that the candidate understands not only what the solution is required to produce but how their solution will be suitable in the given context. |
| Candidate has listed the selected software. | Candidate has attempted to justify the selected software in relation to client needs. | Candidate has fully justified the selected software in relation to the client needs. | |

Take each of these rows in turn, starting with row 1. When an assessor reads the portfolio, the first thing that they want to know is what the portfolio is all about. Who is the client? If they just get something like Version 1 in the box on the next page, then they really will not have any confidence that the student has any idea what it is that they are supposed to be doing.

## Sample descriptions of organisations

### Version 1

Mr Jeffs works for a company that hires out cars. He needs a system that will allow him to keep a record of all of the cars that he hires and who is renting them.

### Version 2

I am going to produce a solution for Mrs Jefferies to help her to find out what she should charge for cakes that she makes and to produce bills for her to give to customers. She makes personalised cakes for customers for special celebrations like birthdays and weddings. She makes about five cakes a week, except near to Christmas when she will make about 20 cakes every week in November and December. She is now thinking of taking on some help and wants to make sure that the solution could manage to work with at least 20 to 30 cakes all the year round.

### Version 3

The Evergreens is the name of an organisation for active retired people. It was started in 2004 by a recently retired gentleman, Mr Wilson, who wanted to organise activities for himself and his fellow retirees who felt that they were, 'far too young to become couch potatoes!'. The organisation currently has a membership of around 200 people and is expanding all the time. The original purpose of the organisation was for pleasure, but more recently the membership has expanded and there is a demand from members to take an active part in local politics. Miss Davies is the secretary of the club and she doesn't really want to spend all of her time in sorting out the members, their subscriptions and bookings for activities. She says that she is just a volunteer and wants to get out there, and not be stuck at home doing paperwork. Miss Davies is my aunt and she has asked me if I can find an easy way for her to store details of members and the activities in which they are interested. She would like to be able to email letters quickly, informing the right people about particular events and be able to produce lists of members with particular interests to give to people organising demonstrations or visits to places of interest, etc.

## TASK 15

Consider the three different descriptions.

1. What mark would you award each of them for row 1 of the table on page 139?
2. What information is missing from the one that you think is best?
3. How could it be improved?
4. How could the student have found out more information?

Row 2 of the table on page 139 is concerned with the actual tasks that the solution has to perform. There is only one of the sample descriptions that really contains any information about the requirements of the solution, rather than just a general overview. But has the student provided a 'list of tasks'?

## TASK 16

If you were a teacher, what advice would you give to the student looking at the Evergreens club to help him/her to gain three marks for row 2?

The client's requirements may sometimes be a little 'woolly' when they first give them to you. They often do not understand what software can do. It is then up to you to tease out exactly what their requirements are and from these you can produce a list of tasks that the solution must be able to complete. For example, a client may say that they want to have an efficient invoicing system. That won't help you much, but if by questioning them you find out that this means that it has to:

- produce a printed invoice
- save a copy of invoice details
- store all customer details
- store details of products
- produce lists of all paid and unpaid invoices

then you have a list of tasks. To gain higher marks you would then have to take each task in turn and describe it in more detail, in such a way that you show that you know exactly what has to be achieved, when and by whom. This is where you may wish to include sample documents to show the sort of thing done now and what is required. Never include these without annotating them or including a description of them in the text. If you just stick them in somewhere in the portfolio, or even worse, add them in to an appendix, they are worthless. This is because you won't have shown what you gained from them.

**HILL HOUSE LIVERY STABLES**
**LIVERY AGREEMENT**

Client details
{
Name of Client: ..................................................................................
Address: ..........................................................................................
Telephone Number: ...........................................................................
}

Horse details
{
Name of horse/pony: ..........................................................................
Sex: ........................................ Colour: ...............................................
Age: ........................................ Height: ..............................................

Any allergies/special conditions we should know about: ..........................
........................................................................................................
........................................................................................................

Feed: AM: ............................... PM: ...................................................
........................................................................................................
........................................................................................................
}

Shows the details about the client, the horse and the contract between the client and livery owner.

Client details
{
Name of veterinary surgeon: ...............................................................
Telephone number: ............................................................................
Name of farrier: .................................................................................
Telephone number: ............................................................................
Insurance company: ...........................................................................
}

All of the details are INPUTS.
{
Type of livery: ...................................................................................
Monthly rate: .....................................................................................
Terms: ...............................................................................................
........................................................................................................
}

Liveries are accepted on the following terms and conditions. Prior to taking up occupancy these terms shall be accepted by the client by signature.

**TERMS AND CONDITIONS**
1   All fees are payable monthly in advance. Extras, i.e. warmers, lessons, clippings, etc. will be billed in arrears.

**Figure 3.39** Blank sample document

---

**HILL HOUSE LIVERY STABLES**
**LIVERY AGREEMENT**

Name of Client: ROSE JONES
Address: 3 CARTER CLOSE, KINGSDOWN
Telephone Number: 03254 763590

Name of horse/pony: GILBERT
Sex: Gelding                          Colour: Bay
Age: 9                                Height: 15.2 hh

Any allergies/special conditions we should know about: Allergic to hay

Feed: AM: Sports Mix                  PM: Same as AM
         2 scoops

Name of veterinary surgeon: R.M. Hazlehurst
Telephone number: 07982 536748
Name of farrier: Bert Black
Telephone number: 02345 769738
Insurance company: NFU

Type of livery: Full ?
Monthly rate:
Terms:

Liveries are accepted on the following terms and conditions. Prior to taking up occupancy these terms shall be accepted by the client by signature.

**TERMS AND CONDITIONS**
1   All fees are payable monthly in advance. Extras, i.e. warmers, lessons, clippings, etc. will be billed in arrears.

**Figure 3.40** Sample document containing real data

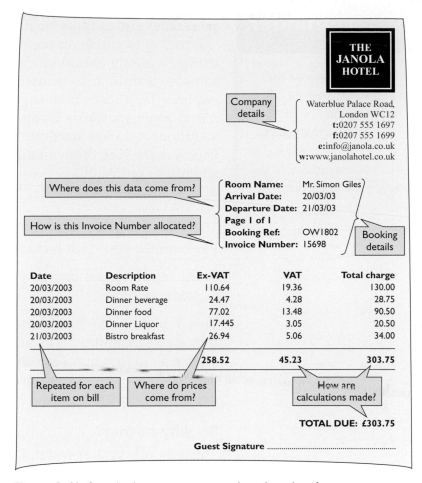

**Figure 3.41** Sample document annotated to show key features

**Figure 3.42** Even a page from a diary can be a sample document

## reminder

Make sure that you give the name and version of the software that you are going to use. This will be influenced by what software the client has to use with your solution and will also determine what features you will have available.

This leads on very easily to the next section on inputs, processing and outputs, or IPO for short.

Row 3 of the table on page 139 is looking to assess the student's ability to understand why relational database software is suitable to be used for the required tasks. This requires the student to understand what relational database management software is capable of doing and in what situations it is most suitable. Your teacher will have helped you to make sure that you have chosen a sensible situation/organisation/task to look at so, if you do understand RDBMSs these marks should be fairly straightforward to gain!

## Input, output and processing needs

Very simply, you must include:

■ the input, output and processing requirements for the solution.

This is one aspect which students often do very badly because they make assumptions as to what is needed rather than bothering to find out. Also, they often do not provide enough detail because they cannot see any marks allocated to this aspect of the project alone.

### So why bother?

The reason is so that you understand what you are trying to do. You will lose marks on A03 if you don't, and it is quite likely that you will produce a solution that won't be acceptable to your client. If you were working commercially and were paid by results, you would become bankrupt or be fired!

### Finding out the IPOs

This is an integral part of being able to describe a task. Remember the whole point of an information (ICT) system is to take input as data and process (convert) it into output (information).

Input (Data) → Processing (Converting) → Output (Information)

**Figure 3.43**

An example of good and bad descriptions of an input, a process and an output is shown in Figure 3.44.

Often, the easiest place to get the information for the inputs and outputs is from the sample documents that you collect. It

| Poor description | Better description |
|---|---|
| INPUT: Customer details | Customer first name |
| | Customer surname |
| | Name or number of house |
| | Street |
| | Town |
| | Postcode |
| | Telephone number (home) |
| | Telephone number (mobile) |
| PROCESS: Calculate total cost of bill | Get sum of cost of all items |
| | Calculate VAT at current rate |
| | Display VAT |
| | Add VAT to sum of cost of all items |
| | Display total with VAT = amount owing |
| | Copy amount owing to next gree line on invoice summary sheet |
| OUTPUT: Report of videos overdue | Header of name of store, and date and time report produced |
| | Sorted by number of days oversue, descending, subheadings for number of days |
| | Page numbers (if multi-page) as footer |
| | Including customer surname, customer number, video code, and video title in tabular format |

**Figure 3.44** Good and bad descriptions of IPOs

is important that you also find out not just what the inputs are – as listed above – but what format they are required in, the range of values they can accommodate, and where the data come from. For example, if the input data are customer details, who enters the details and where do they come from? The customer? If the customer has a customer number, what possible values can this be and, if this is entered, should the rest of the customer details be automatically looked up from a data table? Is this lookup a process?

The range of possible values for a data item is what will help you to determine the format required and any validation rules that need to be built in to your solution. So if you don't have this information you will struggle to gain marks on A01 and A03.

The **processes** are more difficult to find out about and frequently people forget to explain these to you. For example, if you went into a builders' merchants to buy three bags of sand and two bags of cement the assistant would probably just tell you that was £16. He would not say, 'I looked up the price of the sand in the catalogue and multiplied it by the number

## reminder

Do **not** skimp on the time spent on this part of the work. If you do skimp, it will just take longer to do the rest. Also, you need the detail obtained from the study of the inputs, processes and outputs to complete the design work – and remember, the design work is where the highest proportion of the marks are awarded (28 out of the total 70 for this unit).

of bags wanted. Then I looked up the price of the cement in the catalogue and multiplied that by the number of bags wanted. Then I added the two subtotals together to get a total amount!' This means that when you find out what outputs are required you then have to work back to what processes are needed and what data are required to obtain them.

Where the data come from may be important if there is already a stock list or a customer list that you can import and use in your solution. It could be that if this is the case the format of the data that you can use is fixed. In the same way if an output required has to be in a particular format for sending electronically or if a document has to be generated to include particular details so that it can act as an electronic order, the format of the output may also be fixed.

## Design and implementation work A01 and A03

As this unit is concerned with your producing a solution that meets the needs of the client, a lot of the evidence that you need to provide is based on your being able to justify what you have done, and why. This is what the assessment objective A03 is all about – applying your knowledge and understanding to the specific solution you are producing for your client. This is what makes it so important that you have not made up your client and that you have found out enough background information about the client to be able to justify your designs and implementation. The list below shows just what you have to provide:

■ Evidence of, and justification for, the data structures, types and formats used in the solution.
■ Evidence of the:
  – input methods used, i.e. forms, including how the correctness and validity of data is ensured
  – processing, i.e. queries used, calculations made
  – outputs, i.e. forms and reports
  – features, including error messages, that improve the usability of the solution and its suitability for the client, and explanations of how these meet the client needs.

Much of this evidence will be found in your design work, along with annotations to the designs, which include the justification. The person assessing your work will be looking for things like:

■ why you have used drop-down lists as opposed to free text entry
■ why an input form has the fields laid out in a particular order
■ why you have designed a reorder report so that each supplier is on a new page.

It is most important that when you are checking your work you make sure that you have explained all of the design decisions that you have made based on the client needs.

The following table shows some examples of the sort of thing that you might be including:

| Feature used | Justification |
|---|---|
| Format of stock number field set to XX99 (two letters followed by two numbers). | Stock numbers can only be in the range AA01 to XX99. This will prevent inaccuracies in data being entered into the stock field when an employee is querying the stock list or when new stock items are added or deleted. |
| Drop-down list used for customer to select an item of stock from a description, not a stock number. | Customers will be able to select the stock based on a description of the item. Customers will not know stock numbers and if they were left to enter descriptions they would enter many different things. These entries would be hard to validate because they would be free text |
| Stock reorder report contains date produced. | An important requirement of the client was that these reports could be stored in date order so that the date the reorder was sent to the supplier could be checked when making sure new stock has arrived and chasing deliveries. |
| Company logo and title of solution – 'stock reorder system' – appears on every screen in the solution. | This is so a user will always know which application they are using at any time they are working. This is important when people are answering phones or are called away from their desks. |

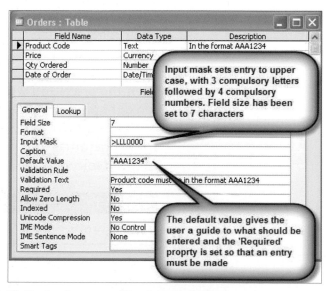

**Figure 3.45** Design features of Product Code field

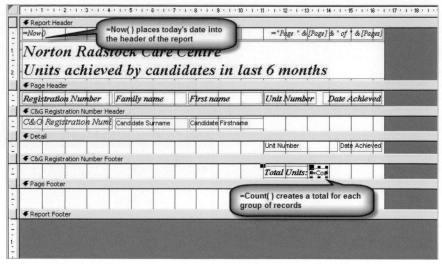

**Figure 3.46** Report design showing field that generates the current day's date

We will now look at the different elements that you need to provide evidence of in order to gain marks on A01 and A03, in a logical order.

## Input

| 1 mark | 2 marks | 3 marks | 4 marks |
|--------|---------|---------|---------|
| Candidate has shown some evidence of consideration of the inputs needed. | Candidate has considered what inputs are needed. | Candidate understands what the input needs of the client are. | Candidate fully understands what the input needs of the client are, including where the inputs are to come from. |

This row is concerned with assessing whether you understand what inputs are needed to meet the client needs and where they come from. For example, a clerk may enter a customer's postcode and then the address and full customer details will be automatically looked up from a file of customer details. Similarly, a customer might enter the description of a product, then the price and whether it is in stock will be automatically looked up and retrieved from the stock list (stock table).

There are various ways in which you can document the inputs required and your teacher will probably suggest a good method for you to use.

## TASK 17

Find out what is meant by an IPO chart or diagram.

## Data types and formats

From an understanding of what inputs are needed and where they come from, you can then go on to design and justify the data types and formats that you are going to use. Marks for this are allocated in A03 as shown in the following table:

| I mark | 2 marks | 3 marks | 4 marks |
|---|---|---|---|
| There is little evidence of the data types or the data formats used. | Ranges of data types and formats have been used but they are not all suitable for the solution. | The data types and formats used have been specified and are suitable for the solution. | Candidate has explained how the data types and data formats used are suitable for the solution. |

These marks are not for the implementation of data types and formats, but for the design of what is needed. This means that you should not include annotated printouts of tables for your evidence here. The evidence may be in a tabular format but **not** a printout.

The following table provides some examples of what you might include as evidence:

| Input needed | From where | Values | Notes | Type and format |
|---|---|---|---|---|
| Customer title | By user at keyboard | Mrs, Mr, Miss, Ms | Only these allowed | Text, maximum size 4 |
| Size of item | From stock file | XS, S, M, L, XL | Only these allowed | Text, size 2 |
| Number of items ordered | By user | 1–99 | Orders over 99 of an item should not be allowed; values of 0 should not be allowed | Number, no decimal places, 2 digits only |
| Date of order | System | Day of order | Date must be automatically generated to provide accurate record of when an order was placed | Date as dd/month/yyyy so that it is easy and quick to read, and day and month cannot be confused |
| Price of item | From stock file | Not specified | Default value is zero | Currency with 2 decimal places |

Once you have implemented your tables you will need to provide evidence for A01 as outlined in the next table. This assessment objective is assessing whether or not you have actually implemented the data types and formats as required for the solution.

| I mark | 2 marks | 3 marks |
|---|---|---|
| Simple data types used. | Range of data types used with appropriate formats. | Range of data types used with appropriate formats with explanation of appropriateness for this solution. |

Notice that you are expected to use a range of data types and formats, so make sure that your solution allows you to do this, otherwise you are restricting the marks that you can achieve.

To provide evidence that you have done this you can produce screenshots as proof. You will need to annotate these to explain how they are appropriate. Do not include lots of printouts. However, you will need to show the data formats as well as the data types. This will require you to do some cutting and pasting from screenshots if a lot of different formats are used. It may be possible to use these as evidence for setting validation rules as well. Figure 3.47 gives an example of how you could achieve this.

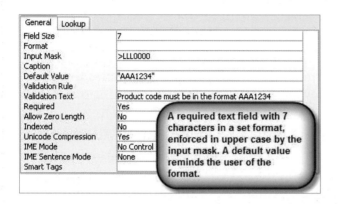

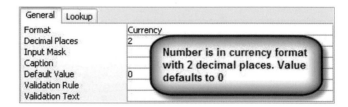

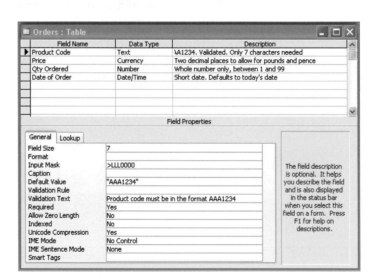

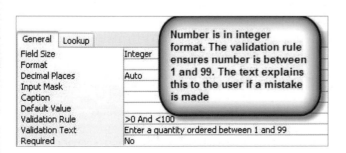

**Figure 3.47** Evidence of data types and formats set up in a data table

## Validity and correctness of data

Of course simply designing the data types and formats for input data is not enough. You must also ensure that any data entered are valid and correct. Marks are awarded for proving that you understand this principle, as shown in the following table:

| I mark | 2 marks | 3 marks | 4 marks |
|--------|---------|---------|---------|
| Candidate has shown evidence of consideration of the importance of the validity **or** correctness of data inputs. | Candidate has shown evidence of consideration of the importance of the validity **and** correctness of data inputs. | Candidate has explained how they have ensured the validity and correctness of data inputs and has shown understanding of the importance of ensuring correct **or** valid data are used. | Candidate has explained how they have ensured the validity and correctness of data inputs and understands the importance of ensuring correct **and** valid data are used. |

Notice in this row that you must consider both the validity and correctness of the data input to be able to gain more than one mark. Look back to page 112 to make sure that you understand what these terms mean and how you have ensured them in your solution. You need to describe this in your portfolio.

Figure 3.48 shows a simple validation rule for a date field – it checks that the date entered is not in the future. If an invalid date is entered, the validation text is displayed.

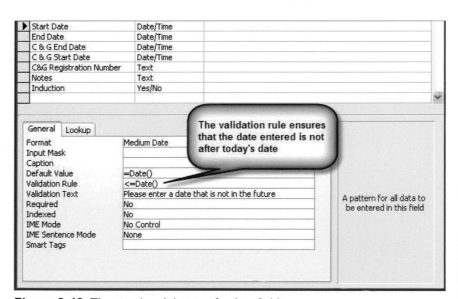

**Figure 3.48** The simple validation of a data field

Figure 3.49 shows how you can set up a verification procedure to display a message when you try to delete one record that has related records attached. To understand this, consider what would happen in a library database if you attempted to delete the record for a borrower who had several books on loan – records for these being stored in a different table, along with the borrower's identity.

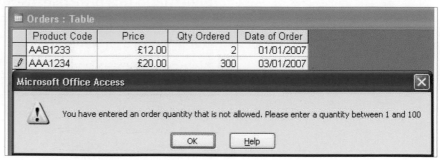

**Figure 3.49** Verification – a message will come up if you try to delete records that have related records attached

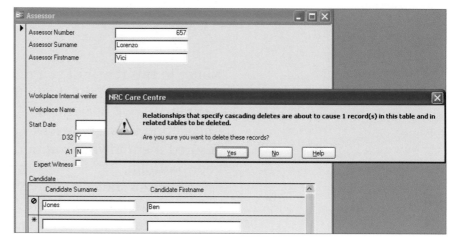

**Figure 3.50** Error message that is displayed when you try to delete a record that has related records attached

## Data structures

Once all your tables are set up, in order to create your data structures you need to implement the relationships between the tables. These relationships should be established as part of the design process and illustrated using a diagram similar to the ones shown on the next page. Now you should include a printout to show that you have actually implemented the design.

A printout would look like that shown in Figure 3.51. This shows the relationships between the three tables that make up a database for a library. The Borrower table and the Loans table are linked by the BorrowerID. There will be one entry in the Loans table for each book borrowed. The Book table and the Loans table are linked by the AccessionNumber.

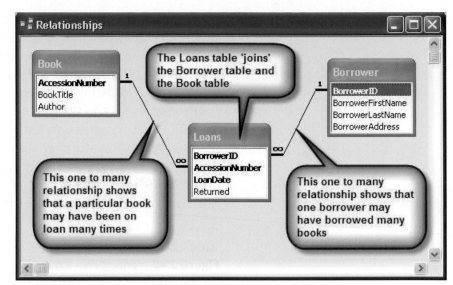

**Figure 3.51** The relationships between the three tables that make up a database for a library

To obtain the top mark in the row of the marking scheme shown below, you need to explain how the data structures used are suitable. This means that you need to show your understanding of the importance of removing many-to many relationships in a relational database structure. This was described in more detail on pages 107–8.

| 1 mark | 2 marks | 3 marks | 4 marks |
|--------|---------|---------|---------|
| There is little evidence of the data structures used. | The data structures used have been specified but are not suitable for the solution. | The data structures used have been specified and are suitable for the solution. | Candidate has explained how the data structures used are suitable for the solution. |

## Processing

Processing is all about something happening to, or being done with, the data that are entered into or stored within the solution. When any type of query is run, processing takes place. Processing needs to be designed. For example, when a customer wants to find out whether an item is in stock, this is achieved by using a query. However, the following processing is involved to achieve this:

- Get description of item
- Match description to stock item in stock list
- Find the number of items in stock
- If stock number is greater than 0
  - display message: 'item is available'
- If number in stock is 0
  - display message: 'sorry out of stock of this item at present'.

This is a simple description using what can be called 'Structured English' to explain what processing needs to take place. Anyone who wants to work in programming, or really be at all successful using ICT as a practitioner, needs to be able to break down processes into this level of detail.

The design for the processing is what will gain you marks for AO3, as you can see in the next table. The assessor needs to see that you understand what processing is required to produce the solution for your client.

| I mark | 2 marks | 3 marks | 4 marks |
|---|---|---|---|
| The solution includes little processing of data. | The solution shows that the processing of data takes place. | Candidate has included processing in their solution that meets the needs of the user. | Candidate has clearly explained how the processing included in their solution meets the needs of the user. |

The implementation evidence that you have actually created the queries comes under AO1, as shown in the following table:

| I mark | 2 marks | 3 marks |
|---|---|---|
| Processing of data takes place to produce outputs. | Appropriate processing of data takes place to produce outputs. | The candidate has shown how the processing of data will take place and how this meets the client needs. |
| Simple queries, for example select queries based on one field, have been used. | A range of queries based on multiple fields/tables or allowing users to select criteria appropriate to the solution has been used. | The candidate has shown how the queries used meet the client needs. |

This means that you must show the processing that takes place and the queries that you have actually implemented. Remember that output can be shown as information in any of the following ways:

- an onscreen form
- a printed report
- an onscreen report
- a response to an action by the user.

Evidence of queries should include the query grid or SQL produced when you have implemented a query. There should also be evidence that each query that you have used actually works. In order to gain 3 marks you must make sure that you have used a range of queries of different types, not just a lot of different select queries, and that you can explain how the way that you have implemented them meets the needs of the client and/or user of the solution.

The following screenshots are examples of queries and the results obtained from them:

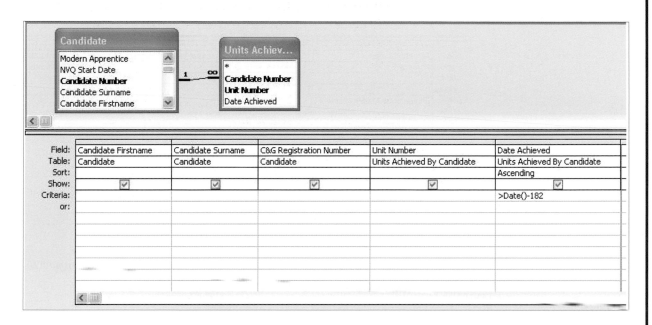

**Figure 3.52** The make-table query at the top takes records with dates that fall in the last six months and sorts them in ascending date order.

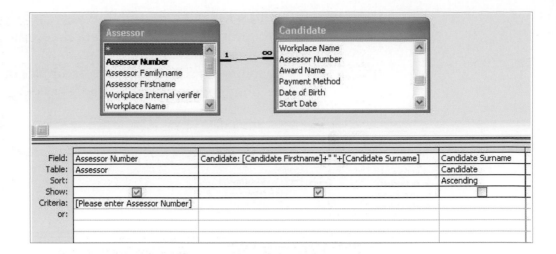

| Field: | Assessor Number | Candidate: [Candidate Firstname]+" "+[Candidate Surname] | Candidate Surname |
| --- | --- | --- | --- |
| Table: | Assessor | | Candidate |
| Sort: | | | Ascending |
| Show: | ☑ | ☑ | ☐ |
| Criteria: | [Please enter Assessor Number] | | |
| or: | | | |

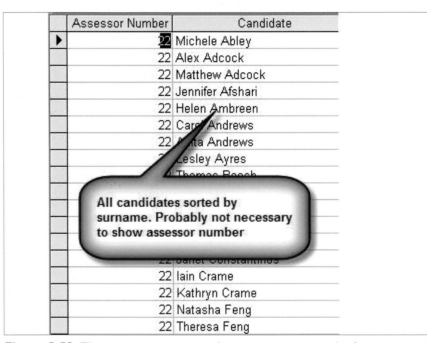

**Figure 3.53** The parameter query at the top concatenates the first name and surname and uses the surname field to sort the results, without showing the surname separately

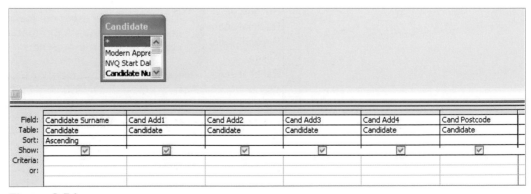

| Field: | Candidate Surname | Cand Add1 | Cand Add2 | Cand Add3 | Cand Add4 | Cand Postcode | |
| --- | --- | --- | --- | --- | --- | --- | --- |
| Table: | Candidate | Candidate | Candidate | Candidate | Candidate | Candidate | |
| Sort: | Ascending | | | | | | |
| Show: | ☑ | ☑ | ☑ | ☑ | ☑ | ☑ | |
| Criteria: | | | | | | | |
| or: | | | | | | | |

**Figure 3.54a**

| | Candidate First | Candidate Surn | Cand Add1 | Cand Add2 | Cand Add3 | Cand Add4 | Cand Postcode |
|---|---|---|---|---|---|---|---|
| ▶ | Michele | Abley | | 231 Franklin Road | Upperby | Carlisle | CA2 9BX |
| | Teresa | Abley | | 15 Walton Road | St Mathias Park | Bristol | BS2 9UP |
| | Dawn Ann | Abley | Flat 4a, Milton Court | behind 13 Ruby Ave | Oldham | Lancs | M45 6QX |
| | Amy | Abley | Golden Cottage | Vicarage Road | Abertillery | Blaenau Gwent | NP13 5TR |
| | Mark | Ackland | | 75 Green Close | Shepton Mallet | Somerset | BA4 7DB |
| | Sandra | Ackland | | 19 Uxbridge Close | Handsworth | Birmingham | B33 6LN |
| | Victoria | Ackland | | | | Oxford | OX4 7GH |
| | Jessica | Adams | | | | Surrey | CR2 5JL |
| | Kathryn | Adams | | | | Notts | NG22 4HA |
| | Samantha | Adams | | | | Cornwall | TR7 5TG |
| | Denise | Adamson | | | | Staffs | ST13 6BJ |
| | Ena | Adamson | | 19 Ebenezer Avenu | Banbury | Oxon | OX16 0HJ |
| | Ann | Adamson | | 7 Derby Road | Sparkhill | Birmingham | B11 5JI |
| | Alex | Adcock | | 23 Wendle Close | Wellingborough | Northamptonsh | NN8 2FR |

*All candidates names and addresses. Refer to Appendix for full printout*

**Figure 3.54b**

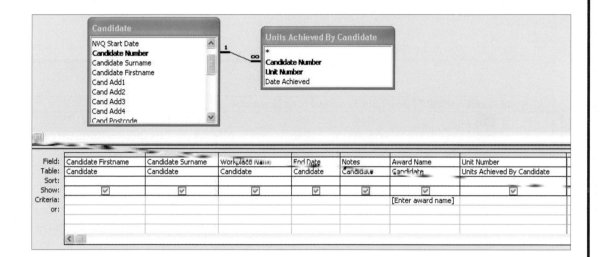

| | Candidate First | Candidate Surn | Workplace Name | End Date | Notes | Award Name | Unit Number |
|---|---|---|---|---|---|---|---|
| | Diane | Feng | Deerhurst Nursing Home | 17/10/2003 | Has all remaining units excep | LEVEL2 | Z9 |
| | Diane | Feng | Deerhurst Nursing Home | 17/10/2003 | Has all remaining units excep | LEVEL2 | ZB |
| | Diane | Feng | Deerhurst Nursing Home | 17/10/2003 | Has all remaining units excep | LEVEL2 | Z6 |
| | Diane | Feng | Deerhurst Nursing Home | 17/10/2003 | Has all remaining units excep | LEVEL2 | NC12 |
| | Diane | Feng | Deerhurst Nursing Home | 17/10/2003 | Has all remaining units excep | LEVEL2 | CU1M |
| | Diane | Feng | Deerhurst Nursing Home | 17/10/2003 | Has all remaining units excep | LEVEL2 | CU10 |
| | Diane | Feng | Deerhurst Nursing Home | 17/10/2003 | Has all remaining units excep | LEVEL2 | CL1M |
| | Elizabeth Anne | Patel | Home Care Brunel Care | 14/05/2005 | Has to complete 3 units (tbc) | LEVEL2 | Z9 |
| | Elizabeth Anne | Patel | Home Care Brunel Care | 14/05/2005 | Has to complete 3 units (tbc) | LEVEL2 | ZB |
| | Elizabeth Anne | Patel | Home Care Brunel Care | 14/05/2005 | Has to complete 3 units (tbc) | LEVEL2 | Z6 |
| | Elizabeth Anne | Patel | Home Care Brunel Care | 14/05/2005 | Has to complete 3 units (tbc) | LEVEL2 | Z1M |
| | Elizabeth Anne | Patel | Home Care Brunel Care | 14/05/2005 | Has to complete 3 units (tbc) | LEVEL2 | CU1M |
| | Elizabeth Anne | Patel | Home Care Brunel Care | 14/05/2005 | Has to complete 3 units (tbc) | LEVEL2 | CU10 |
| | Elizabeth Anne | Patel | Home Care Brunel Care | 14/05/2005 | Has to complete 3 units (tbc) | LEVEL2 | CL1M |
| ▶ | Elizabeth Anne | Patel | Home Care Brunel Care | 14/05/2005 | Has to complete 3 units (tbc) | LEVEL2 | 01M |

**Figure 3.55** In the parameter query at the top of this figure, the user enters the award name and the relevant details are selected from the records that are found

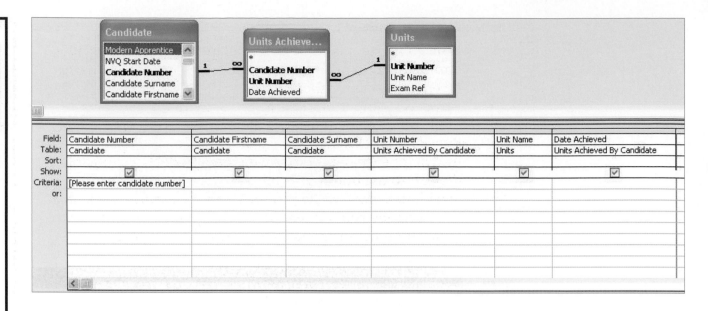

| Field: | Candidate Number | Candidate Firstname | Candidate Surname | Unit Number | Unit Name | Date Achieved | |
|---|---|---|---|---|---|---|---|
| Table: | Candidate | Candidate | Candidate | Units Achieved By Candidate | Units | Units Achieved By Candidate | |
| Sort: | | | | | | | |
| Show: | ☑ | ☑ | ☑ | ☑ | ☑ | ☑ | |
| Criteria: | [Please enter candidate number] | | | | | | |
| or: | | | | | | | |

| | Candidate Num | Candidate First | Candidate Surn | Unit Number | Unit Name | Date Achieved |
|---|---|---|---|---|---|---|
| ▶ | 2535 | Lee | Afshari | B3 | MANAGE USE OF FINANCIAL RESOU | 14/02/2006 |
| | 2535 | Lee | Afshari | C10 | PROMOTE CHILDREN'S SENSORY AN | 12/01/2006 |
| | 2535 | Lee | Afshari | C13 | MANAGE THE PERFORMANCE OF TH | 12/01/2006 |
| | 2535 | Lee | Afshari | C8 | SELECT PERSONNEL FOR ACTIVITIE! | 02/03/2006 |
| | 2535 | Lee | Afshari | D4 | PROVIDE INFO TO SUPPORT DECISIC | 14/02/2006 |
| | 2535 | Lee | Afshari | O3 | DEVELOP, MAINTAIN & EVALUATE S` | 14/02/2006 |
| | 2535 | Lee | Afshari | SC 15 | DEV & SUSTAIN ARRANGEMENTS FC | 12/10/2005 |
| | 2535 | Lee | Afshari | SC20 | CONTRIBUTE TO THE PROVISION OF | 12/01/2006 |
| ✳ | (AutoNumber) | | | | | |

**Figure 3.56** The parameter query at the top gets the user to enter the candidate number and the other data fields are taken from records in related data tables

Never just put a screenshot in without making sure that you annotate it clearly to show what it is providing evidence of. There is more guidance on screenshots in Section 4.

## TASK 18

Write down a description of the following processes using Structured English:

1   Finding the details of a customer given the customer number.
2   Producing a reorder report for all items with a stock value of less than 10.
3   Generating a list of people who have not paid their subscriptions to a club (subscription paid is stored as a Boolean field).
4   Producing a list of all members of a club between 20 and 40 years of age (be careful – the age of a person should never be stored in a database, just their date of birth).
5   Answering the question, 'What is the address of the customer Miss Rosie Wilson?'.

## Error messages

While a solution is being used and processing is taking place, errors can occur. These are caused by the user doing things incorrectly, often without realising that they have done. This is why it is so important to keep users informed of what is happening and to give them clear instructions. All too often designers neglect the issue of the interface until they find out that no one will use or even buy their product because it is difficult to use and makes the user frustrated! Try to get into good habits now, while you are learning. Always think about the language you use and how easy it is for someone else to understand the instructions you are giving to them.

### TASK 19

Remind yourself of the rules for interface design by looking at **Item 10** on the CD-ROM.

The assessment includes marks for showing that you can customise error messages and make them suitable for your intended user. These marks are shown in the following table:

| 1 mark | 2 marks | 3 marks | 4 marks |
|---|---|---|---|
| Only evidence of 'standard system' error messages is provided. | Error messages have been customised. | Candidate has used error messages that are suitable for the users of the solution. | Candidate has explained how they have used error responses that are suitable for the users of the solution. |

It is easy to lose marks by simply using system generated error messages. Most error messages that are system generated are not easy for users to understand and don't give them information as to what to do to prevent the error. It is possible to change the wording of error messages so that they inform and help the user. Your solution should show evidence of your design and implementation of error messages that provide this help to the users of **your** solution.

Here are some examples of good and bad error messages:

**Figure 3.57** Error message that is customised but not helpful

**Figure 3.58** Error message that is helpful

**Figure 3.59** Error message that is helpful and explicit

## Outputs

| 1 mark | 2 marks | 3 marks | 4 marks |
|--------|---------|---------|---------|
| There is evidence of at least one output. | There is evidence provided of several outputs, but these have not been tailored to meet the needs of the user. | Candidate has produced outputs in their solution that have been tailored to meet the needs of the user. | Candidate has clearly explained how the outputs included in their solution meet the needs of the user. |

It may be that you have decided to show your evidence of what outputs are produced by your solution and the different processes in it at the same time as showing the inputs required. This is often the easiest way to do it. Again, there are two sets of marks available:

- for the design of the outputs (see the table above)
- for the use of the report facilities of the software that you are using, showing that you have actually created your reports using more than just the report-writing wizard (see the table opposite).

It is important that you produce good designs for the reports or forms, which will form part of your solution. All too often marks are lost here, not through a lack of understanding of what to do, but because students can't be bothered to produce something accurate and detailed, and instead put in rushed, sketchy designs that a third party could not implement.

**Item 42** on the CD-ROM shows two sample designs: a good one and a poor one.

As with most items, the highest mark is only available if you can show how your report matches the client needs. The mark scheme for reports is shown in the following table:

| I mark | 2 marks | 3 marks |
|---|---|---|
| Simple reports, for example using wizards only, have been used. | Customised reports have been produced. | The candidate has shown how the reports produced meet the client needs. |

> **reminder**
>
> **Third party designs** means that someone else should be able to take your designs and implement exactly what you would have done.

> **reminder**
>
> Remember why Data Protection legislation was introduced – see Unit 1.

> **reminder**
>
> A good way to keep the data secure is to have data in columns in a spreadsheet that you can then sort by column in different ways so that you mix up the names, addresses and phone numbers.

### Security

One thing mentioned earlier is the need to keep data stored and managed using RDBMS both safe and secure. This is because such data are often valuable or of a personal nature. For example, if a marketing database were lost it could be hard to reproduce; if the information is personal, there are legal implications for the people storing it.

When you are working on this unit you must be very careful that you follow the principles of Data Protection legislation. In particular if you are given 'live data' by your client for testing, which includes personal details of real people, you must keep that data secure. Any data that you create should be realistic rather than real, e.g. it should not contain real telephone numbers or addresses.

One of the rows in the marking grid for A01 is concerned with how you have considered security aspects and whether you understand why they are required. You will notice that backing up and passwords are both mentioned in the table below:

| I mark | 2 marks | 3 marks |
|---|---|---|
| Candidate has only superficially considered any security aspects. | Candidate has shown evidence of adopting appropriate security measures, such as backing up and using passwords to protect files. | Candidate has explained the security measures that they have taken and why they are needed. |

## Testing and evaluation

If this is the third unit that you have completed, then you should be getting used to what is required for evaluation criteria, test plans, testing and evaluation.

### Evaluation criteria

You are expected to produce evaluation criteria for the solution in the same way that you did for your newsletter in Unit 1 and the report in Unit 2. These are to enable judgement of how well the solution will meet the client needs. You can only produce your evaluation criteria after you have a clear idea of:

- what the solution you are going to produce will have to do
- how the client wants the solution to work/be used
- the characteristics of the people or person who will use it.

This is so that you can select the most appropriate style and means of producing the required information, for example produce output formatted as an onscreen report or as a printed report. The evaluation criteria are statements about what your solution should **do**, and not what it should contain. These criteria are what you should test your solution against and what you will use to assess the success or otherwise of your solution in your evaluation.

They should **not** be a list of requirements or of the elements you have got to put together. The following table shows some examples of what are not and what are acceptable as typical criteria:

## reminder

Qualitative criteria are opinion-based, whereas quantitative criteria can be measured.

Which of the acceptable criteria in this table is quantitative and which are qualitative?

| Not acceptable | Acceptable |
|---|---|
| The solution should have three tables. | The solution should allow the most effective storage of data that minimises redundancy and allows efficient processing. |
| The reorder report should be a multi-page report. | The reorder report is required with a separate page for each supplier to aid in dispatching requests to suppliers. |
| There should be a parameter query. | It should be possible to find the address of a customer by entering the customer's postcode. |

One thing that is worth thinking about when you write your evaluation criteria is how you are going to test your solution against them. This will affect not just the marks for the criteria and testing, but also the quality of your evaluation.

If you produce criteria like the ones in the left-hand column of the table and simply test the solution yourself, making comments, you will be lucky to gain even one mark. If you have a clear idea of the purpose of the solution and what it has to achieve, and you understand the difference between qualitative and quantitative evaluation criteria as well as how the solution should be tested against these, then you should be able to get three marks. (Look at the marking grid on page 164.)

## Testing

Whenever you are going to be testing a solution, no matter what sort of solution it is, you should always design your testing before you start doing it. Testing must always enable you to prove that your solution does what it is supposed to do in the way that it is supposed to do it and that you can evaluate the solution against your evaluation criteria using the results of testing. The advice given is that you should produce:

■ a test plan to check that the solution meets the evaluation criteria and, therefore, the client needs. The test plan must show what is to be tested and why, the expected results and the data to be used.

Look back to page 133 where advice is given on testing and test plans, and follow these guidelines. You must make sure that as part of testing, your client, or the person who is to use the solution, actually tries using what you've produced. The best way to achieve this is to design some typical tasks for them to complete using the solution and ask for their comments. This is because people who are not ICT experts often find it difficult to know whether or not it is a good solution. However, they would be able to tell you whether it lets them do what they want to do without getting very frustrated, hating the screen colour or being confused by the order of the data entry fields. If you are going to do this, then you need to include some evidence that the client or user has tested the solution and provide a record of what they said. You can use this as proof in writing your evaluation of the solution.

If you run out of time and do not get the chance to do user testing then you should comment on that fact in your time management record and your evaluation of your own performance. This is because it should be an integral part of producing a solution for somebody. If you have missed out user testing this time you should make sure that you **always** make time to do it in your work for other units requiring the production of a software solution.

### reminder

The client and the user may be different people. Think back to the dentist and his receptionist.

## Marking grid for evaluation criteria, testing and evaluation

| 1 mark | 2 marks | 3 marks |
|---|---|---|
| Candidate has provided some evaluation criteria for the solution and carried out some testing. | Candidate has provided both qualitative and quantitative evaluation criteria, some of which are appropriate to assess if the client needs have been met. They have tested the solution against the criteria. | Candidate has identified qualitative and quantitative evaluation criteria that are appropriate for assessing whether client needs have been met and testing takes full account of the evaluation criteria. |
| Candidate has attempted to evaluate the solution. | Candidate has evaluated their solution and identified some strengths, weaknesses and areas for improvement. | Candidate has evaluated their solution and successfully identified strengths, weaknesses and areas for improvement. Candidate draws meaningful conclusions and has made appropriate changes to the solution as a result. |

Notice from the marking grid that marks are not gained for just producing evaluation criteria or for simply putting a test plan into your portfolio. It is the testing process and the evaluation of the solution that are assessed.

When you do an evaluation, you must do it logically, referring to the criteria that you have set and the testing that you have done. To do this logically you should do the following:

- Look at each evaluation criterion in turn.
- Ask yourself:
  - Has this been met or not?
  - Where is the evidence to show whether or not it has been met?
  - If it hasn't been met, why not?

If you write up your evaluation of the solution in this way, taking each criterion in turn and quoting evidence or reasons for success or failure, then you are more likely to produce a good quality evaluation.

This is a straightforward part of the work on which to gain marks. What moderators do not want to see is the student who just states 'I think' or 'as you can see it meets the evaluation criteria' without showing any real understanding or providing evidence to back up what they are saying.

## Planning, time management and evaluation of your own performance

There is guidance included in both Units 1 and 2 on time planning and management (see pages 35–7 and 81–3). In this unit there are a total of six marks available for your description of the actions that you have taken to carry out the work (described as actions taken to solve the problem) and the quality of your time planning and management (as mentioned on pages 136–7). This is what is meant by 'your own performance' (see grid below).

| 1 mark | 2 marks | 3 marks |
|---|---|---|
| Candidate has provided a brief description of actions taken to solve the problem. | Candidate has described actions taken to solve the problem. | Candidate has clearly described actions taken to solve the problem and shows a clear understanding of what they have done and why. |
| Candidate has shown limited evidence of time management or planning. | Candidate has shown some evidence of time management and planning. They have met some of the deadlines and have shown that they understand the need to monitor their progress. | Candidate has shown strong evidence of time management and planning, fully monitored their progress and met deadlines. Reasons for any missed deadlines have been explained. |

The record should show where you got behind, or in front of, your time plan, and how you adjusted it to take account of delays or spent the extra time you found you had.

Be honest! The exam board is looking to see whether you have learnt from what you have done. For example, many students often underestimate how long it takes to find the information that they need for describing the inputs, processes and outputs required or for getting the detailed knowledge of the data formats and validation rules needed.

## Written expression

As in other units, the standard of your written expression is assessed. In this unit, this is concerned with how well you understand the technical terminology of relational database design and implementation and whether you can use the terminology correctly. Also, when this unit is marked you will be assessed for the language you used for error messages or any instructions to users – these should have been written using appropriate terminology for the user. In other words, you'll be assessed on whether you can express yourself clearly in the most appropriate manner.

### reminder

If you look at the examination board website, you will probably find the date that the board expects the marks for portfolio work to be in. It is no use thinking that you have all of the time up to then because the marks have to **arrive** by that date and your teacher will have all of their marking and administration to complete before they can send off the marks. So listen to the date that the teacher gives you!

## Management

Under the Assessment Objective AO1 you will be assessed on how well you have managed your work. (See the extract from the marking grid at the bottom of this page.)

When you produce a database solution, you have to design and implement a lot of separate 'elements' that together make the whole solution. Actually managing these so that you perform tasks in a logical order and know exactly how each item implemented relates to its design, and how these items all fit together, is important in this sort of work. The bigger and more complex the solution, the more important the management aspect becomes. Some database solutions require tens of different queries to be created and without a suitable way of naming these it would be impossible to tell what each one did. This would make it very difficult for someone else to come along and amend a query at a later date or even for the developer themselves to actually find the query that they wanted to do some more work on, or to link to a form.

> ## important note
>
> One of the purposes of providing a key is that a naming convention should be easy for others to understand and allow consistency through the database solution.

### TASK 20

Search in books or on the Internet for what a naming convention is and find examples of appropriate naming conventions used in ICT.

Make up your own naming convention and if you think it needs it, then provide a key.

You need to provide evidence that you have organised and managed your work, so use sensible names for elements of your solution like forms, queries and reports and not ones like query1 and form2! The next table shows the mark scheme for the management aspect of this unit:

| I mark | 2 marks | 3 marks |
|---|---|---|
| The work shows only basic evidence of being managed. | The work has been managed effectively. | Candidate has shown clear evidence of understanding the need to manage their work and has done so effectively. |

## Finally

Put your work together in a logical order and check the following:

- All printouts are readable.
- All work is annotated appropriately.
- Your name and candidate number are included.
- Pages are numbered.
- You have evidence to support everything that you have done.

▶ This section of the book is designed to help you with all of the units in which you have to produce a portfolio. In fact this really means every unit that you take, whether you are on a single AS award course, a single A level course or a double award course. This is because even for the externally assessed units (1, 9 and 10), the work that you have completed still has to be presented as a portfolio.

The following table shows all of the units and indicates which ones you need to complete for which award. The units shown in bold are the externally assessed units; the remainder are internally assessed.

| Box 1: AS User units | Box 3: AS Practitioner units |
|---|---|
| **Unit 1: ICT and society**<br>Unit 2: ICT and organisations<br>Unit 3: Data handling | Unit 4: ICT solutions<br><br>*Plus any two of*<br>Unit 5: Fundamentals of programming<br>Unit 6: Computer artwork<br>Unit 7: Creating a website |
| Box 2: A2 User units | Box 4: A2 Practitioner units |
| Unit 8: Project management<br>**Unit 10: Advanced spreadsheet<br>        design**<br><br>*Plus any one of*<br>Unit 12: Publishing<br>Unit 14: Interactive multimedia | **Unit 9: Software development**<br><br>*Plus any two of*<br>Unit 11: Communications and<br>        networks<br>Unit 13: Systems analysis<br>Unit 15: Supporting ICT users |

Not everyone enjoys doing courses that are assessed through the production of a portfolio of evidence, but it is the best way to be able to show what you are really capable of. If you take an examination, then who knows how you are going to feel on the day and you don't get the chance to go back and improve your answers when you have had time to think about them.

Portfolio work allows you to reflect on what you have done, get advice and improve your work. The mark that you get is a true reflection of the amount of effort that you have put in.

# Why is portfolio work used for assessment?

▶ Put simply, portfolio work is the best way of assessing what you are capable of. When you get to this level of study it is not just about remembering facts. It is also about being able to use what you know and have learnt in different situations. This means that when you move on to higher education or employment you can put what you have learnt into practice. There are also some skills – like time planning, implementing and testing solutions – that cannot be tested very effectively through written examinations. After all, ICT is about using technology to solve problems, so examiners want to see if you can do just that.

Remembering facts is often a waste of time when the important thing today is that you know where to go and find things out – this is something that is assessed in this course, in particular in Units 1 and 2.

# Paper-based evidence

▶ For this course your portfolios have to be produced on paper rather than electronically. There are lots of practical reasons for this:

■ Firstly, preparing a portfolio for electronic submission often means that students spend too much time fiddling around getting things in the right format, rather than concentrating on the content, and so lose marks.
■ Secondly, it can be difficult to do things like annotations or producing rough design work electronically without it taking an awful lot of time, which you will not have.
■ Thirdly, the examination board will **not** accept material in an electronic format because this can constrain the software that you are able to use.

# Being organised

▶ What is important when doing any type of portfolio-based work is that you are organised and that you keep your work in order. You also need to think carefully about the time that you have available and make sure that you don't leave too much to do and end up with too little time to do it in. This is just the same as in an examination where you have to avoid spending too much time on one question – otherwise you might end up not being able to complete all of the questions that you are required to answer. The only difference with portfolio work is that the time available is longer. This often means that people think they have got lots of time and don't need to do much to begin with! These are the students who fail to complete their work.

In this course you will find that for all of the units that you do there are marks awarded for planning and organising your work and in each section there is specific guidance on doing this for the individual units. Do learn by your mistakes. If on the first unit you run out of time and don't get your evaluations written or don't have time to test your work, learn from this experience and make sure that you plan your time more carefully on the next unit so that this doesn't happen again.

**Figure 4.1** The tortoise and hare approach to preparing a portfolio of work

## reminder

There is an example of part of a time plan on page 36 that you can use to help you draw up your own.

Always remember that there are marks for every part of the portfolio and that failing to complete things like testing and evaluation can result in you not being able to gain the best possible mark and hence the best grade. The student who does this once will hopefully learn from their mistakes, but the student who keeps doing it will drive their teachers mad. This is because they will see someone who is probably quite intelligent throwing away marks because they are not being organised!

So once you know what you have got to do, how much time you have available to do it in and any deadlines that your teacher may have given you, do your overall time plan. At this stage you may not know in detail what you are going to develop but you can fill in the development time in more detail later, once you have completed your designs.

Make sure that you know the final date for handing in your portfolio to your teacher and remember that this will be some time before the examination board deadline.

# Understanding what you have got to do

▶ Over the years, I have taught thousands of students and one of the main reasons for students failing to do well in coursework of any kind is that the student doesn't understand what they have got to do. So it is up to you to make sure that you do understand what is expected of you. If it isn't clear to you when your teacher explains it to you, or you feel you aren't sure about something, then **ask**. You will probably think that you have been told to do this for many years, but why is it so important?

Firstly, if you don't know what to do then you can't possibly hope to get good marks. Also, often when students don't know what to do, they just do nothing!

Secondly, when you move on to higher education, or start work, you will find that you need to ask questions because, unlike your teacher, people will tend not to tell you everything that you need to know. So having the ability to be able to think 'what do I need to know', 'who can I ask' or 'where can I find out', is vitally important.

# Where to start

▶ Make sure that you have got a **copy of the specification** for the unit that you are studying. If your teacher doesn't give you one then you can find one at:
http://www.aqa.org.uk/qual/gceapplied/ict.
The specification sets out exactly what has to be covered in each unit and what you need to learn to be able to do (skills), to know and to understand. Often, because specifications are not always written in the most understandable language, your teacher will give you something else to help you!

Here is the list from the specification for Unit 3 – Data handling:

**(a)** A description and justification of how a computerised relational database could be used by a particular client.
**(b)** Evidence of consideration of data types, formats, structures, input, processing and output requirements for a relational database solution to meet the identified client needs.
**(c)** A database containing two related tables has been created to meet the identified client needs.
**(d)** Annotated queries and reports used to search for and present information to meet the client needs.
**(e)** Evaluation criteria and a test plan.
**(f)** Results of testing, which will be used to evaluate the database against the client needs.

(g) An evaluation of work.

(h) An evaluation of own performance.

(i) Evidence of using standard ways of working.

(j) Evidence of appropriate written communication throughout the portfolio.

You will notice that the wording here is more or less the same as the specification, but not the same as that included in Section 3 of this book. This is because the book tries to describe these elements in more understandable terms. If you want a checklist of what must be included, this is your starting point, but notice, for example, that item (b) doesn't tell you what sort of evidence to include. This is where this book and your teacher will help. They will both explain what is meant by these terms and what you actually need to do. The above are 'summary phrases'.

The next step is to find out what you actually have to produce, in what form, and finally, how this will be assessed. In each of the sections of this book you will find links (or references) to **marking grids** that have been provided by the examination board. These are probably what your teacher will use to mark the internally assessed units.

The externally assessed units, past candidate booklets and marking schemes are available on the AQA website: http://www.aqa.org.uk/qual/gceapplied/ict and can also be purchased in paper format from the AQA publications section.[1]

If you are working on one of the units covered in this book, read the relevant section before you start, or read the specification and marking grids, then make a list of what you have got to produce and what needs to be done to produce the required items – this will then form the start of your planning.

# Assessment of all units

▶ All of the Applied units for any of the awards are marked out of 70 marks. They are all assessed against the four assessment objectives:

- AO1 Practical capability in applying ICT
- AO2 Knowledge and understanding of ICT systems and their roles in organisations and society
- AO3 Application of knowledge, skills and understanding to produce solutions to ICT problems
- AO4 Evaluation of ICT solutions and your own performance

---

1 AQA Logistics Centre (Manchester)
Unit 2, Wheel Forge Way,
Ashburton Park, Trafford Park,
Manchester M17 1EH

## So what do the assessment objectives mean?

### A01

This is concerned with your practical use of ICT tools and techniques – for example, how well you can use a piece of software. Do you use the software functions correctly? In Unit 2 you have to make use of styles, headers and footers, footnotes, indexing, etc. – all the functions of the software used to produce reports. In Unit 8 you use the functions of word processing software that allow you to work collaboratively with other people on documents.

### A02

This is about assessing your knowledge and understanding. It carries the highest weighting in Units 1 and 2 where you are looking more generally at how and why ICT is used and the effects its use has on organisations and society. It is not as heavily weighted in the other AS units where you are looking at specific problems. In these units it is concerned with assessing whether you have done your investigation work thoroughly and can see how and why to use the particular software for the particular client and their problem.

At A2 this assessment objective has the lowest weighting.

### A03

This is all about you showing that you can apply knowledge, understanding and skills to a particular problem. It is about using ICT in the most effective way. In most of the units your design work provides a lot of the evidence needed to meet this objective. It is where you will need to gain good marks at AS, particularly to get a good overall grade.

### A04

At AS this only carries 14 of the possible 70 marks but at A2 it is 28 of the possible 70 marks. This reflects the idea that you should be learning how to do evaluation at AS but should be much more competent at the A2 level. At A2, your A03 and A04 marks will very much determine the grade that you get, so when you are taking the AS units make sure that you really understand what is involved in proving you can do these things. You will then be well prepared for your A2 level work.

## How the assessment objectives are weighted

The next table shows the different weighting for each of these assessment objectives across the seven AS units. This allows you to compare the importance of different assessment objectives between units.

| Assessment Objective | Unit 1 | | Unit 2 | | Unit 3 | | Units 4–7 | |
|---|---|---|---|---|---|---|---|---|
| | Marks | Percentage | Marks | Percentage | Marks | Percentage | Marks | Percentage |
| A01 | 18 | 25 | 21 | 30 | 18 | 25 | 21 | 30 |
| A02 | 24 | 35 | 21 | 30 | 10 | 15 | 14 | 20 |
| A03 | 14 | 20 | 14 | 20 | 28 | 40 | 21 | 30 |
| A04 | 14 | 20 | 14 | 20 | 14 | 20 | 14 | 20 |
| | 70 | 100 | 70 | 100 | 70 | 100 | 70 | 100 |

## important note

Figures have been rounded to whole numbers.

In this table the highest percentages are highlighted for each unit.

- In Unit 1, A02 carries the highest percentage of marks – this is for the content of the newsletter or web pages.
- In Unit 2, the highest percentages are for A01 – how well you use the software to produce your report, and A02 – how well you understand how and why ICT is used by organisations.
- In Unit 3, the highest percentage is for A03 – applying your skills, knowledge and understanding to design a solution that meets the needs of a client. In other words, you must produce a highly customised solution.
- For Units 4 to 7, the key objectives are A01 – the use of the tools and techniques, including software, and A03 – applying your skills, knowledge and understanding to designing a solution that meets the needs of a client.

## Common elements of assessment

Throughout all of the units that make up the different courses, certain things are assessed because they are seen as being essential for people taking an ICT course and working with ICT. These are known as 'standard ways of working'. There are many aspects to these, including health and safety issues that should be considered, acceptable ways of naming and storing data files and procedures to follow. In this course each unit assesses slightly different aspects of the standard ways of working. This means that you need to look in the marking grids for where 'standard ways of working' appears and ask your teachers if you are unsure or they haven't mentioned them. What is assessed in Units 1 to 3 is mentioned in the individual sections of this book.

The other thing that is assessed throughout the work that you do at both AS and A2 standard is your written communication skills – being able to write in an appropriate manner for the audience, and communicating using correct English and grammar. You may not think this is particularly important when talking to your friends and family, but it is **very** important when you are communicating with clients as part of this course or once you start work, or are producing work that will be read by others. Think about what would happen if you put up a website where the visitors to it couldn't understand what was being said, or where spelling or grammatical errors gave the organisation that owned the site a bad name.

# Developing a solution

▶ Whichever unit you are undertaking (with the exception of Unit 8 – Project management) you will have to produce some sort of ICT solution to a problem. For Unit 2 the problem is your own but in all of the other units a solution has to be produced for a client.

There are stages that are common to the production of any solution using ICT, and once you have undertaken one unit then these should start to become second nature to you. Experienced ICT developers hardly think about them. They just become a standard way of approaching an ICT solution, and this is what you should be able to do by the time that you finish the course. This is particularly the case if you are completing the double award, which is intended for students who want to become ICT practitioners.

## Stages in the systems development life cycle

If you look at textbooks on ICT, you will probably find a diagram similar to Figure 4.2 in many of them – though the names for the different stages may be slightly different. This is called the Systems Development life cycle.

What you need to know is what this means you have to do for each of the stages.

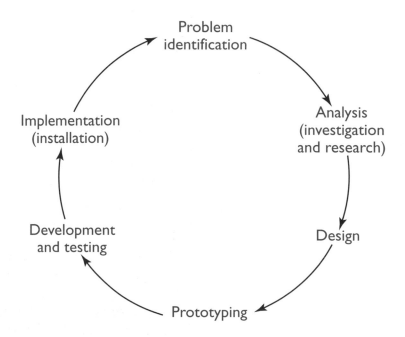

**Figure 4.2** The Systems Development life cycle

## Problem identification

If you were working as an ICT developer, then you would be given problems to produce solutions for by other departments within the organisation you were working for or, if you were working for a software house, by other organisations. For this course it is important that the problems that you tackle are suitable for the unit that you are studying. They should not be so large or so small as to present you with problems in completing the necessary work and in meeting the assessment criteria. This means that you must discuss what you are thinking of doing with your teachers before you start and listen to the advice that they give. They will have attended meetings held by the examination board and will know what is sensible for you to try to achieve in the time available. They will also know how you work and whether something is not going to challenge you enough or alternatively be too much for you to take on in the available time.

This could be compared to the feasibility study stage, when an organisation has to decide whether it is actually possible to produce an ICT solution to a problem.

What is important is that you do have a real client, and this is where your teacher will give you advice on how to find one. So in other words rather than waiting for the problem to come to you, you have got to go out and find one!

## Size of problems v. level of detail

As part of the assessment process at this stage in your education, you have to demonstrate not only that you can do something but also that you understand what you are doing and why you are doing it. For example, if you are using a spreadsheet package to produce a solution for a client, why are you using a drop-down box for the user to make a selection from? Why is this better for the client than the user entering what they want in a blank cell? Examiners do not want to know how you used the software to create the drop-down box, or resize or colour it; they want to know **why** you are using it.

This means that you should avoid problems that are too big, because you need to have a higher level of detail in your work for AS and A2 level than you will have had for GCSE or any other lower level course. Remember, it is quality that is important not quantity.

## Analysis

This is the technical term used to cover the research and investigation stages of a project. This means that you have to do two things:

- Find out as much as you can about the problem and what is required: the outputs, processes and inputs needed.

■ Find out about, and learn how to use, the software that will be needed to produce the solution.

At the end of this stage you should be able to describe what is required and state this as a set of requirements.

These must be checked back with the client to make sure that you have understood exactly what they want. Not spending enough time on this part of the work will mean that you either waste time later or are not able to produce what is wanted. Remember what was said earlier about finding out what you need to produce before you start a unit, and how many students fail if they don't do this – well it is exactly the same here. You need to have a **clear** idea of exactly what the client wants before you go any further.

From your list of client requirements you should be able to produce a set of evaluation criteria for your solution. Look back at any of the previous sections of this book for more information on this aspect. Basically, the evaluation criteria are what you will measure the success or otherwise of your solution against. So they will be needed to determine the testing that you will need to carry out.

### Design

If you find you have trouble producing designs, it will probably be because you have not done enough investigation and so you don't know exactly what the client wants. This is why it is important to make sure that you know as much as you can before you start.

Sometimes with software solutions that are more visual, like ones produced using artwork software or desktop publishing, you may need to go through an iterative process. This means that you need to do a design, show it to your client, get their feedback and then refine the design before showing it to the client again. You will have to keep doing this until you have what they want. Only then do you produce a final detailed design that is exactly what will be implemented.

> ## reminder
>
> Never assume what a client wants. Students who do this rarely get good marks and it is the worst thing that a professional can do.

> ## reminder
>
> ■ In the marking grids it will state how many draft designs you need to include in your portfolio. This is usually given as a maximum number. The draft designs must be included to show how you have gone through the design process and responded to client feedback. You do not have to include lots of draft designs; these will not gain you any extra marks.
>
> ■ These designs are drafts, so they should be neat enough to be readable/understandable by your client and the examiner, but you should not be spending lots of time on drawing them.
>
> ■ If draft designs are produced using a software package, you must state what package was used. Also, for Units 1, 9 and 10, the software used must not be the same software that you are using for your final solution.
>
> ■ Designs should be annotated to show why elements are included and so on – look at the marking grids to check what is needed.

## Prototyping

Sometimes clients do not know what they want because they do not know what ICT is capable of producing. In this case it is often necessary to produce a prototype, developed in or using software, to show them what can be achieved. In Unit 6, for example, you will have to produce samples of artwork to show to your client so that they can select what they like.

## Final designs

Final designs are detailed. They should enable someone else to produce exactly the same solution as you have done by just using your design work. What should be included in the final design is different for different solutions. For Units 1, 2 and 3, the required details are given in this book. For other units you should refer to the relevant marking grids.

In commercial environments, detailed designs are important because often the person who designs a solution will not be the same person who develops and implements it. Also, when changes need to be made to a solution, for example, when new functions are needed by the business, it will be necessary to look back at the designs to see how these changes can be made.

## case study 1

Many of the problems experienced as a result of the millennium – the change to dates starting with '20' and not '19', and the introduction of the euro, were as a result of organisations not having designs for software that they were using. This meant that the programmers who were trying to change the solutions had to spend a lot of time trying to find where dates or currency values were used in the implemented solutions. If designs had existed this would have saved many hours of work and expense.

**Figure 4.3** The Euro was launched in 2002

## reminder

- Designs without annotations gain very few marks.
- Clear designs are worth spending time on.
- Designs need to be present for all of the appropriate elements of the solution. Students often forget to include all of the designs that are needed. For example, designs are often missing for:
  - processes (macros and queries) in spreadsheet or database solutions
  - links and control structures in interactive multimedia or website solutions.

## TASK I

Why is it not possible to carry out comprehensive testing of your solutions? Why do you think you are only asked for sample tests? What problems might you experience with end user testing? What is the difference between an end user and a client?

For your portfolios, detailed design work is important to show exactly what you plan to develop and why you are using particular software functions to meet the client requirements. If you look at the marking grid for the unit you are studying, you will find that many of the marks can be gained from having clear, well-annotated designs.

### Testing

Part of the design for a solution should be the production of a test strategy, test plan and test data. In the development of commercial applications, testing is sometimes outsourced to specialist organisations who can be more objective. However, the design for the testing still needs to be produced.

You must make sure that you do this. Testing and evaluation are given more weighting in the A2 units, but it is important for any ICT solution – unless you have tested a solution, how can you evaluate it?

In the previous sections of this book, there is guidance on testing for Units 1 to 3. However, when you are designing testing in any unit, you should remember the following points:

- Testing is done to make sure that a solution:
  - does what it is supposed to do
  - does it how it is supposed to do it.
- Testing should be against evaluation criteria set as a result of establishing the client needs.
- Testing is carried out throughout the development of a solution, not just at the end.
- Testing may be carried out as part of the design process when rough designs/prototyping are used.
- Testing should be planned. The strategy should indicate what testing will be carried out when, where and by whom.
- Test strategies should describe all testing required, even if, for the purposes of assessment, only sample tests are carried out.
- Test plans should list all tests, the purpose of the test, the expected outcome and data to be used.
- Test plans should, for the purposes of assessment, show a selection of different types of test, rather than lots of the same type of test (for example, validation – see Section 3).
- Testing should involve end users and clients.

Testing to be undertaken by your client and/or users will need to be planned carefully. Don't think that you can simply give them your solution and ask what they think of it. This might get a reply such as 'It looks good' or 'Well it's OK' but they will very rarely tell you exactly what they do or don't like or what they find easy or hard to do. The best thing is to prepare some tasks for the client or user to undertake using the solution that you have produced. This could be something like producing a report, adding some more records, putting their own data into a template, or showing a new logo to some customers. Ask them, for example, what they found easy or hard, whether it took longer than they thought it would or did it save them time?

**Item 41** on the CD-ROM gives some examples of the sort of things that you could get a user to test for a database solution.

### Development schedule

When you have completed your designs, you will know what you need to create and you should try to produce a schedule for developing each of the items that you need. For example, for a database solution you will need to start by creating tables and then set up the relationships between them. At this stage you might decide to add data to the tables and test the validation rules and input masks. You might then create the forms that you need, followed by the queries. For a piece of artwork, you might need to take a digital photograph, manipulate and resize the image to use it as a watermark, insert text on top, and then combine two photographs together by cutting and pasting one onto another.

Basically, you need to work out a logical order in which to do things so that you make the most of the time that you have available. You should also give yourself milestones that enable you to see how well you are progressing. This development plan can be combined with the overall plan for all of your work that you will have done to start off with.

### Development and testing

Once you are clear as to what you have to produce and have the skills that you need to do it in the software that you are using, then it is simply a case of getting on with it. Yes, you may have problems when testing shows that something doesn't work correctly or look right, but you need to persevere, ask for help, use manuals, discuss ideas with other students or staff until you have cracked your problem. This is what many people love about working with ICT – the challenge of getting a machine to do what you want!

Examiners generally do not want to know how you did something using the software, just what you have done. The exception to this is where a unit is concerned with assessing particular skills and you need to show evidence, perhaps by providing validated photographs or witness statements, to show that you have done it. An example is where you have to install items of hardware in Unit 4.

The list of what you need to produce for each unit appears in the specification, and from the marking grids you should be able to see what evidence will be required. You might need to include screenshots or printouts, witness statements or signed-off documents, perhaps even video evidence. (You should note that video evidence is acceptable whereas electronic evidence of other sorts is not.)

You do need to provide evidence of testing and show that you have actually followed your test plan and say what happened during your testing. Sometimes, for example, when you find something isn't working and you have had to change your design or redo a part of it, you may need to include an extra test. Make sure you number your testing evidence to match the test plan. You could also relate the test to the evaluation criteria – this makes it easier to refer to evidence from testing when you are writing up your evaluation.

## reminder

If you are including screenshots or printouts, remember to do the following:

■ Make sure they have a title and relate them to your development plan or design work by using the same names for the item they are showing.
■ Add annotations to highlight what they are showing – use the marking grids to see what they **should** be showing!
■ Annotations should be handwritten – or if typed in, use different fonts, colours or backgrounds to make them stand out.
■ Don't use strange fonts that are difficult to read.
■ Don't make screenshots too small – this puts examiners in a bad mood.
■ Don't make them difficult to read when the portfolio is bound together.
■ If you have used colour in your designs, use a colour printer. However, if you don't have access to a colour printer, clearly annotate your printouts to indicate the colours you have used – and remember to explain why your printouts are in black and white.
■ Use screenshots of file lists that show file size, date created, etc. rather than simply file names or icons.

# Evaluation

▶ Evaluation is a part of portfolios that can easily be forgotten if not built in to the initial time plan. You must get into the habit of leaving time to do the evaluation, both of the solution and of yourself, so that you do not lose marks on this section. At A2 there are 28 out of the total of 70 marks available for work towards Assessment Objective 4 – Evaluation.

The table on the next page shows the weighting for each assessment objective across the eight A2 units.

| Assessment Objective | Unit 8 | | Unit 9 | | Unit 10 | | Units 11–15 | |
|---|---|---|---|---|---|---|---|---|
| | Marks | Percentage | Marks | Percentage | Marks | Percentage | Marks | Percentage |
| A01 | 17 | 25 | 17 | 25 | 17 | 25 | 17 | 25 |
| A02 | 7 | 10 | 7 | 10 | 7 | 10 | 7 | 10 |
| A03 | 18 | 25 | 18 | 25 | 18 | 25 | 18 | 25 |
| A04 | 28 | 40 | 28 | 40 | 28 | 40 | 28 | 40 |
| | 70 | 100 | 70 | 100 | 70 | 100 | 70 | 100 |

You will notice from this table that the weighting for each assessment objective is exactly the same for all of the A2 units and that the highest weighting is for A04 – Evaluation. (The lowest weighting is for A02.)

## Evaluating the solution

This is simply a matter of taking the evaluation criteria in turn, stating whether or not they have been met and how they have been met and providing evidence to support what you say from testing and comments/feedback from your client. They should not be personal comments of the 'I think that' type. This should be approached in a logical, scientific way. If you include comments that start 'I think that', then it is usually fairly obvious that you didn't have a real client or that you never got your client to actually look at or try out what you have produced!

Notice on the marking grids that you don't actually get more marks for saying that the solution works if it doesn't. You are expected to be objective about what its good and bad points are and also be able to say how it could be improved – so don't try to pretend it does things that it doesn't actually do.

## Evaluating your own performance

Honesty is what is needed here. You are meant to be learning from the experience of studying the course and so if you have mismanaged your time say so and try to explain where you think that you went wrong. It could be that it was harder to get to see your client than you thought, or they kept changing their mind about what they wanted, so the designs took longer.

Here are some common mistakes that students make:

- Underestimate the time needed for investigation.
- Think they know the software better than they do.
- Don't listen to advice on the choice of problem so do something that is:
  – too big
  – too small
  – too complex
  – won't show what it needs to
  – has a client who is difficult to contact.

- Make up clients.
- Pretend they have investigated a real problem, when it is all their own idea.
- Don't provide evidence of testing.
- Include too much information in their portfolios because they think volume gains marks.
- Don't explain or think about why they have gone wrong.
- Don't learn from what they did wrong on one unit and make the same mistake on the next unit.
- Don't spend enough time on the investigation and design work because they enjoy working on the computer and don't like talking to people.
- Don't bother to read the specification or look at a marking grid to see how many marks evaluation is worth.

These are just some of the most common mistakes that students make – there are many others, but most of them can be avoided if you simply listen to advice. Teachers are much kinder than employers when you get things wrong!

## When you think you have finished ...

Now is the time to go back and check. If you planned your time correctly then you will have left some time to do this. So what should you be checking?

- That you have included all of the required items in your portfolio – check the specification.
- They are all readable and are easily identified – perhaps add additional header pages to the portfolio to help with this.
- Everything has titles and is annotated to show what you want it to show – check the marking grids.
- The spelling, punctuation and grammar are correct – use the built-in checkers (set to English UK not English US), read it thoroughly yourself and then get someone else to read it.
- Page numbering and a list of contents are present if required.
- The work is in the correct format.
- Evidence of testing and practical activities is clear, and signatures are genuine.
- All sources have been acknowledged so you cannot be found guilty of plagiarism or cheating in any way.
- All pages have your name, candidate number and centre number on them – use headers and/or footers for this.
- There is no unnecessary information included. If you have doubts about the relevance of an item ask your teacher's advice or put it in an appendix, but only do this if you actually refer to the item somewhere in the portfolio. If you can't refer to it you don't need it.
- The portfolio is well bound – two treasury tags or spiral binding are the best, or put it in an envelope folder.

## Finally ...

When you have finished a unit, be realistic. You should be able to tell how well you have done. If you think you didn't do it very well then remember what went wrong and try to improve your performance on the next unit. If you think you did well, then keep going. Always try to achieve the best marks that you are capable of, otherwise you will probably regret it in the future. Try to avoid retaking units unless there is a very good reason why you need to, for example, you simply ran out of time and didn't do any testing or evaluation. This is easy to correct, but going back and redoing a whole unit is really boring!

# Index

Definitions of key terms are denoted by **bold** page numbers; *italic* page numbers refer to figures.